Called to Stand

Reclaiming the Church, the Republic, and the Soul
A Framework for Renewal in an Age of Collapse

Charles Garner

Called to Stand
Reclaiming the Church, the Republic, and the Soul

ISBN: 979-8-9924408-7-4

Copyright© 2026 by Charles Garner and PGS Publishing, LLC

Printed in the United States of America. All rights reserved under International Copyright Law. Contents may not be reproduced in whole or in part in any form without the express written consent of the Publisher.

Acknowledgements:

Scripture references are from the English Standard Version, the New American Standard Version (1977), the King James Version. Any others are noted in the text.

Special thanks to the Wednesday Bunch, whose conversations and insights were instrumental in shaping this volume. I am also grateful to the readers who helped hone its message: Greg Adcock, Dr. Daniel Lambert, Rick Latta, Bill Lincoln, Chuck Lyndh, Dr. David Mitchell, Jim Riley, Tracy Sharp, and Dr. Bruce Speer. Their assistance has been invaluable.

Group Study Guide Available

A free, downloadable Group Study Guide is available at **PGSPublishing.com**. The guide provides a structured, discussion-based formation process for use in churches, men's and women's groups, and civic study groups.

In Tribute:

Dr. Ivan Parke

*Christian gentleman, scholar,
warrior, and witness*

Author's Note

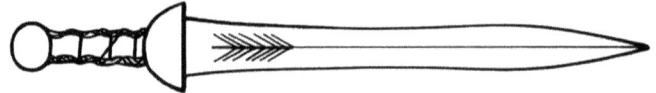

From Reformation to Reclamation

Every generation of believers faces a defining moment—a point when silence becomes betrayal and conviction demands a voice. The sixteenth century had its moment at Wittenberg, when one man's courage broke the silence of a fearful church. We have come to that moment in our generation.

The world we inhabit is different in form but not in nature. The idols have changed their faces; the heresies have traded old robes for new rhetoric; yet the spiritual war remains the same. The enemies of truth are not new—they are the old powers of pride, deception, and fear wearing modern names. It's the oldest lie dressed up in a new suit of clothes.

This book was born from that recognition. It is not merely a chronicle of decline but a summons to recovery—to the church that has retreated, to the pulpits that have grown timid, and to the believers who have forgotten their armor.

We are engaged in a spiritual war in which the very souls of people, the Republic, and the church are at stake. This is not a time for retreat or capitulation. It is a time to practice the disciplines of the faith, to put on the whole armor of God, and — having done all — to stand. We claim the field; we do not abandon it.

The next Great Awakening will not be imported from history; it will ignite in a remnant who refuse to kneel to the spirit of this age and who bow to Christ alone.

This volume accompanies *The Battle for the Republic*, yet it is written to stand alone as a manual for believers who sense the urgency of the moment and desire to be equipped for faithfulness. Together, the two works reveal the full scope of the conflict—its external pressures and its internal preparations.

The time for retreat is over. *Called to Stand* is a call to courage in an age of collapse. The ground may be trembling with the implements of war, but the command still remains:

"Having done all, to stand." — Ephesians 6:13

Charles Garner
Montana, 2025

Editor's Note: Twenty years ago, clarification mattered because access was limited. Today, nearly every reader carries a global library in their pocket. This book is not written to withhold information. Along the way we will mention names, terms, and movements that may be unfamiliar. That is not meant to frustrate you; it is an invitation. When needed, do your own research.

Our task in these pages is to name the patterns and frame the moral stakes, not to turn this into an encyclopedia of dry-as-cracker-dust facts. This is a field manual for warriors. You can often get updated details faster than we could curate them and put them on the page. Some numbers will shift over time—like the fraud case in Minnesota, where totals were still climbing as we wrote—but the patterns remain. Verify what you need to verify. We trust you to do your own work.

Group Study Guide Available

A free, downloadable Group Study Guide is available at **PGSPublishing.com**. The guide provides a structured, discussion-based formation process for use in churches, men's and women's groups, and civic study groups.

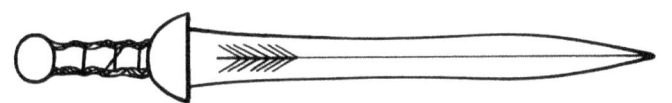

Contents

Prologue   *11*

1: *The Famine of the Word*   *15*

2: *Sheep Without a Shepherd*   *29*

3: *When Generals Fall*   *39*

4: *Transformed not Conformed*   *53*

5: *Reclaiming the Real Church*   *67*

6: *The Priesthood of All Believers*   *87*

7: *Life in the Spirit*   *101*

8: *Seven Disciplines of Personal Discipleship*   *115*

9: *The Trumpet Sounds—Prepare for Battle*   *135*

10: *Rules of Engagement*   *145*

11: *When God Rends the Heavens*   *169*

12: *The Commissioning: When the Church Stands*   *181*

13: *Warrior-King*   *195*

Epilogue   *201*

Appendix   *207*

This is the word of the Lord to Zerubbabel:

"Not by might, nor by power, but by my Spirit," says the Lord of hosts.

Zechariah 4:6

Prologue

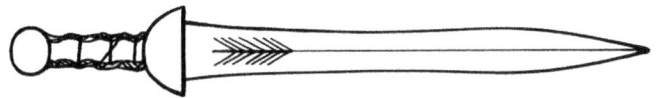

Life in the Spirit
Disciplines of the Christian Warrior

"If you know the enemy and know yourself, you need not fear the result of a hundred battles.
If you know yourself but not the enemy, for every victory gained you will also suffer a defeat.
If you know neither the enemy nor yourself, you will succumb in every battle."
— Sun Tzu, *The Art of War*

We have studied the enemy's ideology and tactics. Now we turn to the army of God itself — its formation, its training, and its tactics. The war that began in ideas can only be won through disciplined lives shaped by truth and empowered by the Spirit.

In the previous volume, we traced the long war against the foundations of the Republic—how ideas captured institutions, how language disarmed conscience, and how enemies within and without worked in concert to weaken a free people. That work was diagnostic by necessity. This volume is corrective by design.

The battle we traced in the culture now comes home to the church. For too long, believers have watched the smoke of battle on distant horizons without realizing the fight was already in the sanctuary. The line between liberty and coercion has crossed the threshold of faith itself, testing pulpits, fracturing fellowships, and revealing hearts. Before the church can stand in a collapsing world, she must first be purified within.

The next movement turns from the outer war to the inner famine—from clash of ideologies to shaping and equipping of the soul of the Christian warrior. Here the Commander begins His inspection, calling His people back to the Word, the Spirit, and the courage to stand when others fall.

The Return of the Prophet's Voice

The assassination of truth always precedes the assassination of people. Falsehood prepares the soil for bloodshed. But this story is not without hope. Every age of confusion has also been an age of awakening. When truth is buried, it waits—not to be forgotten, but to rise.

What was lost through moral cowardice can be recovered through moral courage.

What was compromised by cultural compliance can be renewed through spiritual conviction.

The rebuilding must begin where the collapse began: in the soul and in the sanctuary. Families matter. Schools matter. They are the first classrooms of the heart and the early shaping-grounds of a nation's future. But the decisive battleground—the place where renewal must take root—is the church. For half a century, my calling has been to equip the people of God for the work God has assigned to them, and that calling frames this entire book.

Now we turn to the one institution that still stands as the last guard against collapse.

The Church as the Final Line

Gramsci identified three institutions that must be weakened or eliminated for a society to fall: the family, the school, and the church. A century ago, the long march began threading through all three—each one essential, each one shaping the heart of a culture and the survival of a republic.

But the focus of this work is the church—the Body of Christ, composed of those who follow Jesus. This is the army of God. This is the place where warriors are trained, where truth is proclaimed, where the armor is fitted, and where the battle lines are drawn. The church is not merely the refuge when the walls shake; it is the command post from which the people of God advance.

And the day to stand is not coming. It is now.

Scripture gives us many images of the church: an army, a bride, a building, a flock, leaven, fire, branches, a family. Each teaches something vital about her nature and mission. Yet in this moment, the image of the army is the one we most need to recover. The church is not a retreating remnant; it is a disciplined force under divine command, called to hold the line when others yield.

From Diagnosis to Formation

In the first volume of this companion work, we traced how language was captured, how institutions were softened, and how a century of ideas prepared the ground for bullets. But a field manual cannot end with forensics. If truth has been assassinated, it must be resurrected in the only place revolutions cannot finally reach—the formed soul.

In Scripture, liberty survives not by outrage but by formation: life in the Spirit, practiced disciplines, and an equipped priesthood of believers. If politics is downstream from culture, and culture is downstream from conscience, then the church's work is upstream labor—equipping believers (*katartízō*), issuing armor, and training warriors.

We turn to the forge: not events, but endurance; not performance, but tenacity of purpose; not weekend religion, but daily yieldedness. Here we take up the disciplines of the Christian warrior and the armor of God—training not for comfort, but for conflict; not for admiration, but for obedience; not for show, but for steadfastness.

This is where believers are shaped, where strength is restored, and where the people of God learn to stand in a world that no longer does.

1

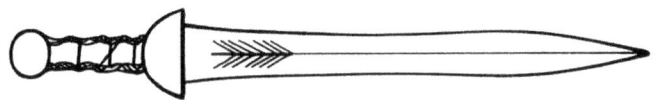

The Famine of the Word

*"Behold, the days are coming," declares the Lord God,
"when I will send a famine on the land—
not a famine of bread, nor a thirst for water,
but of hearing the words of the Lord."* — Amos 8:11

The first symptom of a wounded church is hunger—hunger that is not recognized until the strength to stand is gone. Long before pulpits went silent, hearts grew malnourished on fragments of truth and the sweet syrup of sentiment. The famine does not begin in the streets but in the sanctuary, when the Word that once thundered becomes an echo of itself. What follows is predictable: faith weakens, conscience dulls, and the church forgets how to speak with authority in a world begging for a message from God.

Amos wasn't a professional prophet. He was a shepherd and a gatherer of sycamore figs—a man of calloused hands and open eyes. But when Israel hardened its heart, God sent this herdsman as a sentinel. And he wrote what he saw—a people starving for the word of God.

After Solomon's reign, the nation had divided: ten tribes to the north, two to the south. Yet to both, God sent watchmen— Elijah and Elisha, Amos and Hosea to Israel; Isaiah, Joel, Micah,

Zephaniah, and Habakkuk to Judah. Their message was always the same: **repent before ruin.**

But the people—once blessed—had become self-satisfied. Amos indicted them in a counterclockwise roll call of guilt: Damascus, Gaza, Tyre, Edom, Ammon, Moab, and finally Judah. Their charges were clear and familiar:

- Carnal security — guilty.
- Scoffing at God's judgment — guilty.
- Violence and oppression of the poor — guilty.
- Laziness and idle pleasures — guilty.
- Drunkenness and self-indulgence — guilty.
- Lack of compassion — guilty.

When the Word is rejected, judgment is not far behind. In 722 B.C., the Assyrians swept through the Northern Kingdom, scattering its people, dissolving its tribes. Their cruel genius was dispersion—removing a people's language, memory, and identity. A dispersed people cannot unify; eventually, they lose their history and their name.

Montana Plain: "That's how the Northern Kingdom disappeared. Break a people apart long enough, and they stop being a people. No shared memory. No shared identity. No future. Just fragments that never come back together. And before long, the name itself is forgotten."

The parallels to our own time are deeply unsettling. The prophets spoke into a world much like ours—prosperous, distracted, morally numb. They saw that when nations stop listening to God, He lets them have what they want. *That* is the famine Amos described: not of food or rain but of revelation—a silence born of neglect.

As Joel 3 warns,

> *"The day of the Lord is near in the valley of decision."*

We are living in that valley now. The question before us is simple and terrible: **What shall we choose?**

Entropic Warfare

We are facing entropic warfare, and we have been complicit participants. Entropy is the slow drift from order into disorder. It doesn't strike with force; it erodes with time. That is the warfare we are facing — a quiet unraveling of the foundations that once held our churches, families, and schools together. Our strong foundations have been undermined. We have experienced an infiltration into the institutions that comprise the culture of America—formed by our families, schools, and the church.

Our focus in this volume is the church…specifically, pastors. Our pulpits have been captured by a Marxist, atheistic, pagan culture. It did not come in violent takeover. It came gently, luring with promises of success, it changed the vocabulary and took away the language of God. And it left only the disaster of a weakened church in its wake—one that looked more like the world than it did like heaven.

The Infiltration

Jude described our situation vividly:

Beloved, although I was very eager to write to you about our common salvation, I found it necessary to write appealing to you to contend for the faith that was once for all delivered to the saints. For certain people have crept in unnoticed who long ago were designated for this condemnation, ungodly people, who pervert the grace of our God into sensuality and deny our only Master and Lord, Jesus Christ. —Jude 3-4

The Therapeutic Turn
Our age has its own famine. Churches still fill on Sunday, but the bread has lost its substance. The sermons soothe more than they stir. The Cross is displayed but rarely explained. What used to be a pulpit has become a platform.

The preacher once thundered, *"Thus saith the Lord."* Now many whisper, "Here's how to feel better about yourself." Sermons are measured not by their truth but by their tone. In too many places, we've replaced repentance with reassurance and holiness with happiness.

Montana Plain: "If you sand off all the edges, you don't end up with a shepherd's staff — you end up with a stick that can't guide or guard."

This is not new. Every generation faces the temptation to trade the fear of God for the favor of men. But when the pulpits grow timid, the culture grows loud. A church that once shaped nations now struggles to shape sentences.

From Watchmen to Entertainers
Ezekiel warned the watchmen that if they saw the sword coming and did not sound the alarm, the blood of the people would be on their hands. Paul told Timothy, *"Preach the word; be ready in season and out of season; reprove, rebuke, and exhort, with complete patience and teaching. For the time is coming when people will not endure sound teaching, but having itching ears they will accumulate for themselves teachers to suit their own passions, and will turn away from listening to the truth and wander off into myths* (2 Timothy 4:2-4)."

That time Paul spoke of has come into its fulness in America right now. The modern pulpit has too often chosen polish over prophecy and timidity over boldness. Stage lights have replaced the sacred flame. Pastors quote psychologists more than prophets. Worship has become performance, and sermons have become self-help talks.

Montana Plain: "If the trumpet gives an uncertain sound, nobody knows which way to march."

When the pulpit softens, the people scatter. When the shepherd stops warning, wolves multiply.

The Weight of the Pulpit

James issues a warning that should make every preacher's hand tremble on a Bible: *"Not many of you should become teachers, my brothers, for you know that we who teach will be judged with greater strictness."* (James 3:1)

The pulpit is not a platform; it is evidence. God will play back what we have preached.

A man who ascends a pulpit steps onto a scaffold. The stricter judgment is not about polish, but about stewardship—what we did with God's Word and God's people. James talks about the tongue because a teacher's words can steer a soul like a bit in a horse's mouth… or burn down a soul like a spark in dry timber.

Paul reinforces this in language that leaves no room for soft options: *"I charge you in the presence of God and of Christ Jesus, who is to judge the living and the dead… preach the word; be ready in season and out of season; reprove, rebuke, and exhort…"* (2 Timothy 4:1–2)

He saw a day coming when people would not endure sound teaching, but would gather teachers to tell them what they wanted to hear. That day has arrived. The indictment is double-edged:

- People want soft lies.
- Teachers are willing to sell them.

Many pulpits in our time are no longer guard towers on the wall but vendor stalls in the square. Too many have become hawkers and their people gawkers. They do not stand between wolves and sheep; they run surveys on what kind of wolf the sheep prefer.

This is not a style issue. A pastor who trims the truth to keep a crowd is not "struggling with relevance"; he is inviting a heavier judgment. A captured pulpit is not a branding problem; it is a soul-at-stake problem.

The Shadow of the Woes
We should be careful with our words. Not every weary pastor is a Pharisee. Not every confused leader is a wolf. But Jesus has already spoken to a certain kind of religious leadership in Matthew 23, and His words still burn.

He condemned leaders who loved their titles more than their people, who tied up heavy burdens but would not lift a finger to help, who shut the kingdom in people's faces, who strained out gnats and swallowed camels, who polished the outside and left rot within, who honored dead prophets while silencing living truth.

When church leaders in any age:
- love position more than repentance,
- treat the platform as brand instead of stewardship,
- use the name of Christ to baptize the ideas of the age,
- trade repentance for affirmation and fear God less than losing followers…

—they step into the long shadow of those woes.

We dare not pretend Jesus has nothing to say about such shepherds. The Judge has already published His verdict.

This book is not written to flatter a heroic remnant and simply scold "the culture." It is written to warn us—especially those of us who preach—that God takes our words with terrifying seriousness. If our pulpits have helped produce a generation that cannot stomach truth, then repentance must begin behind the pulpit, not only in front of it.

When the Church Became an Empire
The pattern is as old as history. When the Church forgets its first love, it begins to hunger for control.

After the apostles died, bishops rose in prominence. By the fourth century, political ambition and theological innovation began to intertwine. Jerome, in his *Letter 15 to Damasus* (c. 376–377), flattered the bishop of Rome with language that laid the foundation for papal primacy — claiming authority for the Roman See as Peter's heir. What began as counsel soon hardened into dogma.

Four decades later, at the Council of Carthage in 418, Augustine's teaching on inherited sin was enshrined as canon law. Salvation was declared impossible apart from the Church's sacraments. Grace became a commodity dispensed through clerical hands. The Church of Rome became both priest and prison — the only medium, it claimed, through which Christ could be known.

And through that claim, it held the reins of Europe's kings and the consciences of men. The same institution that once preached forgiveness became the power that sanctioned persecution. What it would not destroy through repentance, it crushed through force.

The famine of the Word deepened — not because Scripture ceased to exist, but because it was locked away. As the prophets had warned Israel, so the early believers learned: when revelation is replaced by ritual, famine returns under new vestments."

The Reformers Who Spoke into Famine

Yet God always keeps a remnant. When the Church lost its way, He raised men and women who loved truth more than comfort and obedience more than approval. They stood when others bowed, and through their courage the Word found its way back into the world.

Peter Waldo, a wealthy merchant in twelfth-century France, read the Gospels and heard Jesus say, *"Sell what you have and give to the poor."* He obeyed literally. He gave away his wealth, learned the Scriptures, and began to preach in the language of the common people. For that, he and his followers — the **Waldensians** — were branded heretics by Rome.

For three hundred years they were hunted, tortured, and burned. They memorized Scripture because owning it meant death. They taught their children in mountain caves and valleys, lighting candles where priests and soldiers would not go. They were poor, powerless, and faithful — a light in the darkness.

When the Church of Rome tried to silence them, they sang psalms louder. Their courage lit a hidden fire that would one day burst into full flame in the Reformation.

Montana Plain: "They couldn't burn the Bible out of them, so they burned the people who carried it."

Two centuries later, **John Wycliffe**, called the *Morning Star of the Reformation*, picked up that torch in fourteenth-century England. He declared that the Church could not stand above Scripture. He translated the Bible into English so even a plowboy could read it. "The authority of Scripture," he said, "is greater than the authority of the Church."

His writings spread to Bohemia, where **John Huss** inspired by Wycliffe, stood in Prague preaching repentance and renewal. He proclaimed the same truth — that Christ, not the pope, is the head of the Church. For that, he was burned at the stake. As the flames rose, he prayed, "In a hundred years, God will raise up a man whose calls for reform cannot be silenced."

A century later, that prayer was answered. **Martin Luther** nailed his 95 Theses to a church door in Wittenberg and stood before emperor and pope saying, "My conscience is captive to the Word of God. Here I stand; I can do no other. God help me. Amen."

William Tyndale, following him, carried the Word across Europe. Under threat of death, he was hunted across Europe for translating the English Bible. Before his execution, he prayed, "Lord, open the King of England's eyes."

The Awakening That Followed
When truth is buried, it never dies—it waits.

In the eighteenth century, **John Wesley** rose from the ashes of cold religion and preached holiness of heart and life. He reignited the dying embers of English faith, riding horseback through rain and ridicule to preach the Gospel. "The world is my parish," he said. "Give me a hundred men who fear nothing but sin and desire nothing but God…and they alone will shake the gates of hell."

Centuries later, voices like **A.W. Tozer** and **Leonard Ravenhill** called the modern Church back from comfort to conviction:

A.W. Tozer revived that same fire in the twentieth century. "We need a baptism of clear seeing," he wrote, "and a fearless declaration that God still reigns." Tozer warned, "A scared world needs a fearless church."

Leonard Ravenhill, in the same generation, thundered, "The only reason we don't have revival is because we are willing to live without it." He was a man who refused to make peace with spiritual drought.

Each of these men — Waldo to Ravenhill — stood against the silence of their time. Each one rediscovered the same truth: the Word of God is not chained, and the remnant never disappears. Each spoke into famine—and rain followed.

Every time the church fell silent, God raised a voice in the wilderness.

The Word cannot be chained, and those who carry it cannot be erased.

The Consequences of Silence
When the church loses its voice, tyrants find theirs.
When pulpits grow weak, politics grows loud.
When preaching loses its fire, society loses its light.

The famine of truth in our day did not begin in Washington — it began in the pulpit. The church lost moral authority long before the culture lost moral clarity. And as before, it will not be restored through strategy or marketing but through repentance and courage.

The prophets of old thundered, *"Thus saith the Lord."*
The reformers declared, "Here I stand."

What will this generation say?

Rebuilding the Pulpit: A Field Manual for Recovery
If famine is to end, the rebuilding must begin where it started — in the pulpit.

God still revives nations through men and women who tremble at His Word. The cure for a captured church is not a new strategy but a renewed stewardship. Every pastor, teacher, and witness must return to the ancient order of battle: Word first, Spirit always, courage at any cost.

1. Restore Expository Preaching
Open the text, explain it, apply it, and let it speak for itself.

A congregation fed on fragments grows weak; a people fed on the full counsel of God grows strong. The pulpit is not a platform for personality, but a desk for revelation. When Scripture is again the main course, the famine ends.

Montana Plain: "You don't fix hunger with frosting — you serve meat."

2. Recover Theological Vocabulary
Words shape worlds.

When churches trade "sin" for "mistakes" and "repentance" for "personal growth," they empty truth of its power. Let the biblical words return: holiness, judgment, mercy, redemption, cross. They may sound hard to modern ears, but they still raise the dead.

3. Retrain the Shepherds
Every soldier returns to the range; every shepherd must return to the fields of prayer and study.

Seminaries teach method; the Spirit teaches fire. Method builds sermons; only God builds messages. Pastors must learn again to wait before they speak — to hear from God before they preach for God. Revival begins when pulpits rediscover the secret place.

4. Recommission the Saints
The pulpit is not the only place truth must stand.

Every home is a small sanctuary; every believer carries a corner of the front line. Equip the people to handle the Word, to speak it, to defend it, to live it. When the pew becomes the second pulpit, the enemy loses ground.

5. Rekindle Holy Courage
Truth without boldness is mute.

The world will always applaud the preacher who flatters it; heaven honors the one who confronts it. Courage is not cruelty — it is love unwilling to lie. Better a small flock with fire than a crowd anesthetized by comfort.

Montana Plain: "If you've got a fire in your bones, it'll heat a whole church."

The famine of truth began when pulpits forgot their purpose. The recovery begins when they remember it.

Rebuilding the pulpit is rebuilding the nation's conscience. Every faithful voice that rises again becomes a watchtower restored, a trumpet refitted, a fire rekindled. The fields are ready, the Word is waiting — it's time to feed the flock again.

The Charge to Stand
Paul's charge still echoes through the centuries:
"Therefore take up the whole armor of God... and having done all, to stand." — Ephesians 6:13

When the world goes dry, the church must dig wells. When truth is mocked, the church must speak anyway.

When pulpits fall silent, even a whisper of Scripture can

sound like thunder. So let it thunder again. Let preachers preach as if souls still matter. Let believers live as if truth still saves. For the famine will end only when the Word returns to the center — not as decoration for our sanctuaries, but as the declaration of our lives.

The famine has run its course. The land is dry, the pulpits are silent—not of words but of authority and power—and the people wander for lack of revelation. Yet every famine carries the seed of awakening. When God shakes a nation, He first shakes His church. What begins as collapse can become correction—if the remnant will rise.

Montana Plain: "When the barn's empty, it's not time to paint the doors—it's time to feed the stock. The herd always goes where the food is."

The famine has revealed a church that forgot how to feed herself. But God never ends a story with starvation. When He allows hunger, it is to awaken appetite. When He withholds, it is to renew dependence. And that renewal rarely begins in crowds; it begins in the single believer, the single pastor, the single congregation that returns to the Word and bows again before the Lord.

Before the church can stand in public, she must kneel again in private. But we dare not pretend the famine has had only private consequences. When shepherds go silent and gatekeepers fail, the sheep do not simply grow thin—they grow scattered. The wounds of the sanctuary soon appear in the streets.

The famine in the house of God has set up a national crisis of shepherdless sheep.

In the chapters that follow, we will look honestly at what happens to a people *"like sheep without a shepherd"*—harassed and helpless, battered by powers they cannot name and leaders they can no longer trust. Only then will we be ready to hear what it means to rebuild devotion, restore discipline, and raise up men and women who can stand when others fall.

Stand to Purpose: The Word as Weapon

• Take one passage this week and meditate until it shapes prayer, not opinion.
• Ask: When did my teaching last cost me comfort? Would I still speak it?
• Pray for pastors to preach with fire, not favor.
• Resolve that the famine ends here—begin feeding daily on the Word.

2

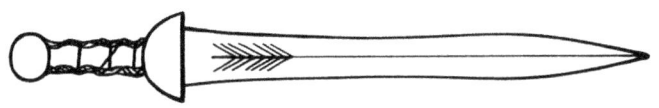

Sheep Without a Shepherd

When Jesus looked across the crowds of His own people—sons and daughters of Abraham, a nation with Scripture, history, and covenant behind them—He did not see strength. He did not see composure. He did not see a people standing tall in moral clarity.

Matthew tells us, *"He had compassion on them, because they were harassed and helpless, like sheep without a shepherd"* (Matthew 9:36). The Greek words for harassed and helpless describe a people *flayed* and *cast aside*—bruised, bewildered, pushed about by forces they could not control and leaders they could not trust.

It is striking how Jesus' diagnosis echoes the prophets. Ezekiel had said centuries earlier that Israel was scattered because their shepherds had failed—leaders fed themselves instead of the flock, and the people wandered into danger (Ezekiel 34:5–8). Jesus saw the same affliction in His day: a nation spiritually malnourished, morally disoriented, and led by men more interested in prestige than truth. Their scattering was not accidental; it was the predictable consequence of failed shepherds.

That same image reappears at the darkest moment of Jesus' ministry. On the night of His arrest, He told the disciples, *"You will all fall away... for it is written, 'I will strike the shepherd, and the sheep of the flock will be scattered'"* (Matthew 26:31). And they were. Fear dissolved their courage. The flock fled because the shepherd was struck.

Scripture gives us this pattern repeatedly:

> **When shepherds fail—or fall—the sheep scatter.**
> **When shepherds stand, the sheep find strength.**

That biblical pattern mirrors the sober social pattern unfolding in our own generation.

Nine Steps Toward Civil Breakdown

In a recent broadcast, Glenn Beck outlined nine steps by which modern nations slide into civil conflict. He was responding to Joe Rogan who made a comment upon hearing the reactions surrounding the death of Charlie Kirk.

Rogan confessed that he believed America might already be around "step seven" on the steps toward civil war. Beck's list was not fearmongering—it was diagnosis. And when laid beside Scripture's shepherding metaphor, the parallels are startling.

Civil conflict does not begin with bullets. It begins with **failed shepherds**. It begins when those tasked with guarding truth, justice, and unity abandon their post. It begins with those tasked to guard and defend against the wolves are silent before the slaughter.

Here are the steps that were outlined:

1. Loss of civic trust

Every conflict begins when people stop believing the system is fair. We have crossed this threshold. Republicans distrust elections. Democrats distrust the Supreme Court. Independents distrust everything.

Lebanon walked this road in the 1970s. *Yugoslavia* walked it in the 1980s. *Venezuela* walked it in the 2000s.

Where trust collapses, the flock is already wandering.

2. Polarization becomes identity

Disagreement is survivable; identity conflict is not. Americans now sort themselves by ZIP code, values, news sources, and tribe.

That's how *Rwanda* descended into madness. Identity eclipsed humanity. People scattered, fearing others.

3. Failure of the gatekeepers

Gatekeepers—those tasked with shaping values, channeling truth, and restraining harm. The gatekeepers in our culture—media, educators, political parties, civic institutions—are supposed to restrain the extremes. Today they amplify them.

Beck said, "The referees have left the field." Scripture would put it another way: **the shepherds have neglected the flock.**

4. Parallel information realities

Civil wars do not need different opinions—only different realities.

- In Lebanon, newspapers for each sect reported different versions of the same events.
- In Rwanda, radio created a fictional world that justified slaughter.
- In America, algorithms have built digital universes where neighbors no longer share truth.

Sheep hearing different voices wander in opposite directions.

5. Loss of neutral rule of law

This is the pivot point. When justice becomes partisan, collapse accelerates.

Venezuela and Yugoslavia crossed this line long before violence erupted.

Ezekiel warned that when shepherds pervert justice, the flock scatters into exile.

6. Normalization of political violence
Violence stops shocking. Threats become jokes. Mobs become messaging.

This is where Lebanon and Yugoslavia passed the point of return. This is where America hovers dangerously.

Jesus saw the crowds "harassed"—literally battered by forces beyond them.

7. Rise of militias and parallel forces
When trust in institutions fails, people arm themselves with alternative guardians.

Lebanon drowned in militias. Yugoslavia shattered under them. Venezuela weaponized them.

When the shepherd's rod is gone, wolves define the night.

8. The trigger event
No civil conflict begins with a plan—it begins with a spark: a disputed election, a political assassination, a financial collapse. Beck said the room "is soaked in gasoline."

The prophets would say the sheep are already scattered on the hills, vulnerable to every beast.

9. Institutional fracture
When police, military, or federal agencies split, unity is gone. America is not here—but we can imagine it. And the fact that we *can imagine it* is itself a warning.

These steps are not inevitable. They are warnings; signposts, not prophecies. They reveal the path a society travels when its shepherds fall silent and its moral center dissolves. They are not an argument for despair, but a call to vigilance and to repentance.

A nation drifts toward fracture when no one stands in the gap, but it can return from the edge when truth is proclaimed and courage is restored. Collapse accelerates when the church is silent — and reverses when she awakes.

And it doesn't take all of the church. God has never needed a crowd — only a remnant willing to stand. To see God's hand, it only takes a few. Gideon's 300 routed 135,000 Midianites because they each stood in their own place using the weapons and strategy that God dictated. What He did then, He can do today.

Why Jesus' Warning Matters Now

Jesus did not merely diagnose the crowds.
He responded with compassion—and with a call.
"The harvest is plentiful, but the workers are few.
Ask the Lord of the harvest to send out laborers into His harvest." —Matthew 9:37–38

In other words:

- **Where shepherds are absent, God calls new shepherds.**
- **Where leaders are silent, God calls new voices**
- **Where the flock is scattered, God calls gatherers.**

This is the hinge of our moment. This is the core of *Called to Stand*. The nation is not simply politically divided—it is spiritually leaderless. Jesus looked at a nation losing itself and said, *"Pray for shepherds."*

He looked at disciples who would scatter and said He would rise again to gather them. He identified Himself as the Good

Shepherd who lays down His life—in contrast with the hired hands who run when wolves appear (John 10:11–13).

We are living in a Matthew 9 moment: harassed people, helpless institutions, failing leaders, and scattered sheep.

We are living in an Ezekiel 34 moment: shepherds who feed themselves instead of the flock.

We are living in a Matthew 26 moment: sheep who scatter when shepherds fall.

And God is calling His people—pastors, churches, ordinary Christians—to step into the field as laborers when others have fled.

Why the Church Is the Most Fixable Gatekeeper

Beck said something remarkable, **"The easiest one to fix is the church."**

And he was right.

- You cannot easily reform the FBI.
- You cannot easily reform the media.
- You cannot easily reform universities.
- You cannot easily reform Congress.

But a church is a flock under a shepherd. A congregation under Scripture. A pastor with a pulpit and a Bible. A community that gathers around truth, not power.

If the shepherds stand, the sheep will rally. If the pastors speak, the silence will break. If the churches rise, the nation will have a witness again.

This is not wishful thinking. It is the testimony of history. Nations have collapsed—and been rebuilt—because religious courage reappeared when political courage evaporated.

Look closely at the record:

When culture rotted in 18th-century England, it was not Parliament that ignited renewal—it was the open-air gospel preaching of men like George Whitefield and John Wesley. England was drowning in gin-houses, child labor, collapsing family life, and the beginnings of industrial dehumanization.

Reform did not originate in the palace, the courts, or the newspaper halls, but in fields, foundries, coal camps, and farm villages where Scripture was preached plainly to common men and women. That spark did more than save souls—it eventually changed laws, birthed schools, reformed prisons, fueled abolition, and reshaped national conscience.

When America was drifting into a moral abyss in the early 1800s, it was not Congress, the courts, or the governors who redirected the nation — it was a wave of ordinary, Spirit-stirred believers who gathered in barns, brush arbors, riversides, and makeshift camp meetings. The young republic was drowning in alcohol abuse, family breakdown, and widespread atheism among cultural elites.

Yet the fire was rekindled not by legislation but by preaching, testimony, song, and sacrament on the edge of the frontier. The movement did not wait for permission. It simply obeyed heaven, and the culture followed its wake.

> *Sometimes the wind of God begins in a log cabin,*
> *not a legislature.*

When Germany lost its moral spine during the rise of Nazism, the resistance was not first political—it was pastoral and confessional. The Barmen Declaration of 1934 did not come from the Reichstag; it came from a remnant pulpit. When state churches bowed, men like Karl Barth, Dietrich Bonhoeffer, and Martin

Niemöller drew a doctrinal line in the sand: "Jesus Christ, as he is attested to us in Holy Scripture, is the one Word of God... We reject the false doctrine...." In a climate where fear ruled, the only public courage that remained came from men who feared God more than Gestapo standing outside doors at midnight.

When racial apartheid hardened the soil of South Africa, it was not Parliament that broke the stone —it was the preaching and witness of a spiritual remnant. The Confession of Belhar emerged from pastors and congregations who said, "Unity, reconciliation, and justice are not political slogans—they are gospel imperatives." Political structures did not lead that movement—they followed it.

In every case, the turning point did not begin with power but with preaching; not with strategy but with conviction; not with influence but with obedience. Renewal did not flow downward from rulers — it rose upward from the remnant.

These are not museum exhibits; they are case studies in divine strategy. When God wants to turn a nation, He rarely begins with kings. He begins with prophets, pastors, and praying saints. He begins in pulpits no one broadcasts, in prayer meetings no one advertises, and in hearts no pollster measures.

The stage is not D.C. and the actors are not statesmen. Nations shake when pulpits sleep — but history turns when prophets wake. The battlefield is the church and the soldiers are the saints. Out here, we'd say: revival doesn't need a spotlight, it needs a spark.

So yes — the church is the easiest to fix not because it is small, but because its authority does not come from ballots, budgets, buildings, or boards. Its authority comes from:

The Word of God
The Spirit of God
The people of God
The mission of God

And when those four come back into alignment, even the gates of hell lose their swagger.

The Call of This Hour
This chapter is not written as a dirge—it is a summons. A commissioning. A call to take the mantle Christ placed on His disciples when He saw the crowds fainting under the weight of a world without shepherds.

The crisis before us is real. The steps toward national fracture are plain.

But Scripture gives us a deeper truth:
A nation with failing leaders is a nation ready for revival if the shepherds of God rise.

This is the moment for churches to reclaim their purpose. For pastors to speak truth without fear. For believers to stand firm when others scatter. For Christians to be laborers in a field white for harvest. And for the Good Shepherd to lead His people once again—not into panic, but into courage; not into conflict, but into clarity; not into surrender, but into strength.

This book is not meant to merely diagnose collapse. It is to mobilize shepherds. To gather scattered sheep. To teach the flock to stand.

Because Christ still looks upon this nation—harassed, helpless—and His response remains unchanged: Compassion. Calling. And a summons to rise. A command to stand.

"Strike the shepherd, and the sheep will be scattered."
Zechariah 13:7

3

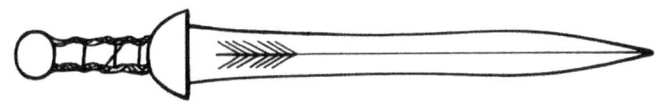

When the Generals Fall

"Do not be conformed to this world…" — Romans 12:2

"Demas has deserted me, having loved this present world."
2 Timothy 4:10

Read this chapter as if you are carrying a torch into a dark sanctuary—not shouting, but weeping, warning, and calling up courage. Let it breathe; it will feel heavy. But hope will rise inside it.

When the Lines Waver
There are moments in war when the front does not collapse because the enemy charges harder, but because commanders fall.

At Chancellorsville, Thomas "Stonewall" Jackson's corps drove like a spear through Union lines. Dusk fell. In the confusion and the trees, his own men misidentified him and fired. Jackson lost his arm, then his life. Robert E. Lee is said to have mourned, "He has lost his left arm; I have lost my right."

The lines wavered not from an enemy surge, but from the loss of the man at the front. The army staggered.

The people of God know that feeling. The enemy studies our ranks. He knows that if he can drop a shepherd, a hundred sheep will scatter. So he aims high.

The church is like an army when its generals fall. The enemy doesn't always charge from without; sometimes silence within announces that the ramparts have failed. Not all deserts are made of sand. Some are made of silence—pulpits gone quiet, shepherds gone soft, watchmen who forgot they were posted on a wall.

Montana Plain: "Some deserts start when the spring quits flowing at the source."

When the spring dries at the pulpit, the valley in the pew starves.

For a century, the long march swept through schools, media, and government. But the bitterest victory came inside the house of God—when shepherds traded a staff for a spotlight, holiness for relevance, salt for sugar. The wolves didn't storm the gate first; they came as consultants, influencers, and experts. They taught pastors to win crowds, not guard souls; to measure ministry by metrics; to confuse mission with marketing. We didn't just grow quiet; we were shaped—pressed into a mold not our own.

"Do not be conformed to this world," Paul warned. The verb is *syschematízō*—don't be pressed like clay into a pagan mold; don't let applause become your compass or flattery your fuel. But we did. And while the faithful sang hymns, the wolves studied **demographics, culture, marketing, theater—the mold of the world**. And they figured how to bring down the generals—they did it with applause. They love applause; they fear authority. But when authority stands without truth, it is only theater.

Before we examine systems, we must look at souls. Collapse is never only structural; it is always personal.

Demas—The Anatomy of Drift

From a dungeon with execution near, Paul wrote: *"Demas has forsaken me, having loved this present world."* Few sentences in Scripture ache like this one.

Demas was no novice. He traveled, preached, suffered, and served shoulder-to-shoulder with the apostle—and still, he drifted. He didn't renounce Christ; he replaced Him. He didn't leap into apostasy; he slid into comfort. The slope is greased with success and the applause of men. The world didn't storm his heart; it seduced it. Paul's partner in mission was lost to the world.

Demas: The Man Who Drifted Toward the Lights

His name first appears quietly, tucked inside Paul's closing greetings from a Roman prison cell: *"Luke, the beloved physician, greets you, as does Demas."* No titles, no commendations, no warnings — just a name alongside Luke, one of Scripture's most meticulous historians. That single mention tells us one thing with certainty: Demas was close enough to the fire to feel its heat. He was not a casual attendee or a curious observer. He was part of Paul's ministry circle, walking near the epicenter of apostolic mission.

Sometime later, Demas appears again — and this time the reference is stronger. Paul calls him a *"fellow worker"* (Philemon 24). That is no small phrase. Paul never handed out that title like a ribbon for participation. To be called a fellow worker meant that Demas had shown himself trustworthy. He had labored, suffered, served, prayed, traveled, endured, and invested in the work of the gospel. He was no spectator; he was yoked to the mission. He likely saw miracles, conversions, demonic confrontation, and the rapid expansion of the gospel into hostile territory. He stood shoulder-to-shoulder with heroes whose statues we would carve if they lived in our day.

But Scripture is painfully honest, and the final mention of Demas drops like a stone: *"For Demas, having loved this present world, has deserted me and gone to Thessalonica."* (2 Timothy 4:10). No farewell. No explanation. No lingering affection. Paul, nearing execution, writes his last inspired words with abandonment still fresh in his pen.

The tragedy is not that Demas left Rome. Others did as well — Timothy went to Ephesus, Titus to Crete, and even Paul sent men out for strategic reasons. The tragedy is why. Demas did not leave because of persecution, threat, imprisonment, or even theological disagreement. He drifted because he fell in love with the world he once renounced.

The devil could not frighten him away, so he learned to attract him away. It was not the lion's roar that conquered Demas — it was the whisper of comfort, convenience, and compromise. This world is full of men who would never deny Christ with their lips, but slowly abandon Him with their loves.

Demas traded eternal reward for temporary relief. He exchanged unseen treasures for immediate pleasures. His story warns us: not all deserters run in fear — some stroll away in fascination. It is entirely possible to walk with Paul, serve with Luke, labor for Christ, and still lose heart if one's affections are not anchored in the age to come.

We do not know what awaited him in Thessalonica. Perhaps wealth. Perhaps reputation. Perhaps family pressure. Perhaps business opportunity. Perhaps the faint glow of a life less demanding. But we know what he lost: the honor of finishing well beside Paul at the greatest hour of witness — when the stakes were highest and the torch was ready for the next generation.

Demas is a reminder that ministry proximity is not the same as spiritual perseverance. Yesterday's faithfulness does not guarantee tomorrow's obedience. He is proof that you can begin with zeal and end with regret; that you can travel with an apostle but not arrive at the crown; that you can labor for Christ and still prefer the world.

His life asks a question of every modern believer, pastor, and leader: *Which love is growing — the love of Christ, or the love of the present age?*

This is not written to condemn Demas — Scripture leaves his eternity in God's hands. It is written to warn us. For the line between a fellow-worker and a deserter is thinner than we think, and no one drifts toward holiness by accident.

Montana Plain: "Up here in the mountains, a man doesn't get lost all at once — he wanders a little at a time."

> May God grant us not only the zeal to begin, but
> the grace to finish.

Demas is not just a name in history—it is a mirror in every generation. Every headline of fallen leadership echoes his tragedy: gifted apologists undone by hidden darkness, global ministries collapsing under secrecy, mega-platforms shattered by moral breaches and silence, hierarchies masking predators, networks excusing performers, and "celebrity pastors" not taken down by attack so much as by ascent to their own platform.

We speak these wounds not to preen, but to grieve, to be sober, and to remember. This is not friendly fire in the fog of battle; too often it is fratricide—a man pulling the pin inside his own tent.

The greatest danger to a leader is not persecution, but prosperity—not the world's hatred, but the world's hug. Preach the word; stand your post; endure hardship. The crown is never given to those who retreat.

Jesus' Woes and the Hirelings

Jesus reserved His sharpest words not for pagans, but for religious celebrities: *"Woe to you, scribes and Pharisees, hypocrites..."* He named them: blind guides, whitewashed tombs, serpents and vipers. Their sin was not a lack of religion, but the weaponizing of it. They loved titles, seating, honor, image. They polished the chalice and left poison within.

He warned again: *"The hireling sees the wolf coming and flees."* The hireling preaches peace when judgment is at the door, calls compromise "wisdom" and cowardice "winsomeness," trimming truth into a palatable shape for men rather than a holy offering unto God. Even now, however, grace waits at the edge of every woe for the one who will repent and return to the Shepherd. Beloved, plain talk: salt stings, sugar sells. One heals; the other rots. You cannot be salt if you are terrified to sting.

The Apostolic Intelligence Briefing

The Spirit told us where the breach would come—from inside the ranks.

Paul warned that savage wolves would arise from among the flock and that in the last days men would love themselves.

Peter said false teachers, driven by greed, would exploit the faithful.

John named the lust for preeminence.

Jude pointed at hidden reefs and waterless clouds.

This is not gossip; it is battlefield intelligence. The deepest wounds are not when the world attacks us, but when those bearing the Name betray His character.

Acts 20—The Shepherd's Oath

Picture Paul, weathered and scarred, on the shore at Miletus addressing the Ephesian elders. He held nothing back. He preached publicly and house-to-house. He warned night and day with tears. He proclaimed repentance toward God and faith in Christ preaching the whole counsel of God. He refused silver, gold, applause, titles, or ease. He did not build a brand; he built disciples. He did not cultivate fans; he trained soldiers.

"After my departure, savage wolves will come in among you," he said—not to pagans, but to elders. They wept because they knew: the battlefield would soon be theirs. And now, it is ours.

Salt That Stings—Jesus' Burning Question

"If salt loses its saltiness... what good is it?" In the first century, Dead Sea "salt" was often mixed with gypsum. If moisture leached the true salt away, only white dust remained—it looked like salt but did nothing. So with the church.

Salt seasons; it changes what it touches. When God's people become identical to the world, witness evaporates. Salt preserves; when it fails, corruption spreads. Jesus warns that such salt is thrown out and trampled—compromise ends not only in ineffectiveness but in humiliation. Truth stings; salt burns in a wound. Refuse to sting, refuse to heal.

The church is not called to soothe culture but to sanctify it. And salt does not lose flavor overnight; it dilutes over time through neglect and contamination. "Salt" is not just a task; it is an identity. Lose saltiness, lose self. You cannot lead toward truth while living in fear of losing applause.

In ancient Israel, salt kept meat from decay. If the very thing meant to prevent rot becomes rotted, what hope remains?

Doctrine: Keel and Ballast

A church without doctrine is a sailboat without ballast. Christ is the keel—the unyielding center beam binding every plank and rib. Without Him there is no ship at all. Doctrine is the ballast—

the weight below the waterline that holds us steady when storms press and currents pull. It doesn't glitter. No one applauds ballast. Remove it, and the first strong wind lays you flat.

Winds of false teaching blow hardest where there is no weight of truth. Many congregations have confused sail for substance—full bands, excited crowds, excellent aesthetics—and almost no ballast below. Storms come suddenly in a world like ours. When they do, it won't be the glittering masts that keep believers upright. It will be the keel and ballast—Christ and doctrine—that keep them from capsizing.

A sermon may fill a room; only doctrine fills a soul with stability. A congregation may admire a gifted communicator; only truth equips saints to stand. Better a humble boat heavy with truth than a shining yacht that capsizes when the wind shifts.

Montana Plain: "A boat without ballast might look fast on calm water—but it'll roll belly-up in the first crosswind."

The Pastor as Equipper—Ephesians 4:11–16
Christ the Giver (v.11). *"He Himself gave…"* The risen Christ is the Giver; leaders are gifts to the people, not owners of them. *Poimenas* and *didaskalous*—shepherding and teaching—belong together. Real shepherds feed (doctrine) and guard (discipline). If a pastor boasts, "I don't preach doctrine," he is boasting that he doesn't feed the sheep.

The Threefold Purpose (v.12). *"…for the equipping of the saints for the work of ministry, for the building up of the body…"* *Katartismós* mends nets and sets bones—doctrine restores function. The saints do ministry; pastors train. Doctrine is scaffolding for growth; without it, the house sags. Pastors who avoid doctrine produce people who avoid ministry.

Targets of Equipping (v.13). Unity is not fog; it is shared content. *Epígnōsis* is accurate, relational knowing of Christ. Maturity means grown-up, not gullible. The goal is Christlikeness, not brand loyalty.

The Storm We're Training For (v.14). Without doctrine, infants are tossed by waves and carried by winds—*kubeía* (dice-play) and *methodía* (scheming) name the cunning and the method. If doctrine isn't taught from the pulpit, it will be taught by the world.

How We Grow (v.15). We are to speak *"truth in love"*—steel and velvet. Doctrine is not arid; it is a map to the living Christ.

The Engine of a Healthy Body (v.16). From Christ the whole body, each part working, makes growth. The pastor's teaching creates supply lines; without them, the body starves at the limbs.

Orders to the Pastoral Corps. Guard the deposit. Devote yourself to the reading, exhortation, and doctrine. Refute those who contradict; teach what accords with sound doctrine. If you will not teach your people, the culture will.

A Plain-Speech Pastoral Checklist. Open Bible, terms defined—sin, repentance, atonement, justification, sanctification, adoption, glory. Confess the non-negotiables—Trinity; Christ's deity and humanity; substitutionary atonement; bodily resurrection; Scripture's authority; salvation by grace through faith. Name the winds—therapeutic moralism, prosperity "gospel," deconstruction-as-virtue, universalism, works-righteousness. Put tools in hands—context, cross-references, the grand story: creation, fall, redemption, new creation. Measure maturity by doctrinal grasp, ministry engagement, and love under truth.

A Word to the "No Doctrine" Pastor: If you don't preach doctrine, what do you preach? Ephesians 4 charges you to equip saints until they are stable in truth and grown up into Christ. Stability requires structure; doctrine is that frame. Refusing doctrine is refusing your tools. It leaves the flock charmingly inspired and criminally undefended. You can't steady saints in a storm without a keel and ballast.

Yet even with clear orders in hand, many still falter—and so the Captain of our salvation allows the shaking to begin at home.

When the House Is Judged

Judgment does not begin in Hollywood or Washington. It begins in the sanctuary. *"Judgment must begin at the house of God."*

Christ cleanses His house not because He is done with it, but because He intends to return to it. When He shakes His people, He saves them. He purifies and separates—shepherd from hireling, wheat from chaff, soldier from spectator—and He raises a remnant. Not famous ones—faithful ones.

The Remnant Rises

In every age, God's heroes are not platformed but planted: a widow intercessor in the back pew, a bi-vocational pastor who never compromised, a missionary who buried friends and stayed, an elderly saint who prayed revival into a young preacher's bones, a deacon who defended the weak, a layman who stood when the pastor fell, a young mother discipling her children, a grandfather teaching men at a diner before sunrise.

When celebrities fell, they stayed. When applause faded, they prayed. When others ran, they rebuilt.

Their keel was Christ. Their ballast was doctrine. Their anchor was holiness. Their allegiance was eternal.

Build Where You Live—Nehemiah's Secret

Nehemiah's wall rose in fifty-two days because each family built the section by their house. Men fight hardest for what shields their own doorstep. Reform is not a press release; it is a hammer in your hand.

Rebuild your section—your marriage, your children, your congregation, your town; your pulpit, your small group, your school board, your business; your intercession hour, your daily Scripture, your repentance. Awakening does not begin in Washington or New York; it begins in living rooms and prayer closets.

The Kingdom advances one obedient household at a time. Rebuilding demands not only tools but leaders who will stay at their post when others fall.

Orders When a General Falls

If a leader falls, grieve—hard hearts don't heal holy wounds. Pray for the fallen—for repentance, truth, and justice. Speak of this with tears, not triumph — these are not statistics, but souls. Guard your heart from cynicism; bitterness is not discernment. Do not despise the office because a man disgraced it. Tell the truth to your people—no spin, no smirk, no savoring. Strengthen the line. Step up. Take responsibility for your sector of the wall. Re-center on Christ and doctrine. Tighten the keel; add ballast.

This is not the hour to retreat. The King has not abdicated. Christ does not resign. When generals fall, the faithful take up the banner.

Reflection for the Flock

1. Where did you first see compromise in leaders—and what did you learn?
2. Which temptations pull hardest on you in this culture?
3. What doctrines keep your keel deep and your ballast heavy?

4. Where is God asking you to stand where others have fallen?
5. Who are the "unknown generals" in your life—how can you honor them?
6. Will you be salt—even when it stings?

Reflection for Staff & Elders
1. Where, specifically, are our people "tossed by winds" right now? Name three.
2. Which core doctrines have we not taught explicitly in 12 months? When will we?
3. How many members are equipped and deployed in ministry (not just attending)?
4. Do our groups reinforce core Christian doctrine, or replace it with sentiment?
5. What is our plan to "speak truth in love" when we must confront popular errors?
6. Where are we tempted to trade holiness for relevance?

Our generation does not need stars; it needs shepherds.
It does not need men who can grow brands, but men who can grow disciples.

A Final Word
Brother, sister—do not fear the shaking. God does not shake what He intends to abandon; He shakes what He intends to strengthen. Christ is not finished with His people. He is purifying His army. And He still calls generals—not those who chase platforms, but those who carry crosses.

    Stand your post.
    Guard the flock.
    Hold the line.
    Advance the truth.

The King is coming, and He rewards those found faithful at their station.

Stand to Purpose: Hold the Line of Leadership
- Guard your post when others resign theirs.
- Refuse applause that costs authority.
- Feed the flock before you feed the crowd.
- Pray for fallen generals and rise to the gap.
- *"Endure hardship as a good soldier of Christ Jesus."* (2 Tim. 2:3)

For whom he did foreknow, he also did predestinate to be conformed to the image of his Son, that he might be the first-born among many brethren.

Romans 8:29

Webster's Bible Translation

But we all, with unveiled face beholding as in a mirror the glory of the Lord, are being transformed into the same image from glory to glory, just as from the Lord, the Spirit.

2 Corinthians 3:18 NASB 1977

4

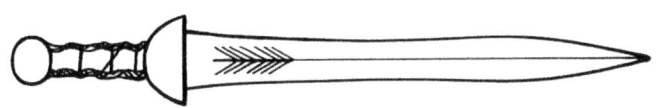

Transformed not Conformed

"Do not be conformed to this world, but be transformed by the renewing of your mind, so that you may prove what the will of God is—that which is good and acceptable and perfect."
(Romans 12:2)

There is a quiet machinery at work in every age—gears grinding, pressure mounting, culture leaning with its full weight upon the soul. It does not always roar; often it whispers. It does not always attack; more often it invites. But make no mistake—the world has a mold, and it intends to press the people of God into it.

Paul did not offer advice here; he sounded a warning. This is battle language, Exodus language, *do not bow* language. And pastors of this hour—shepherds of Christ's flock in a shaking generation—you stand at the fault line where that pressure meets the people of God. If you bend, they break. If you blur, they lose the path. If you soften the note, the trumpet will not summon the saints to stand.

The world presses. But by the mercy of God, we are not molded.

The Pressure of the Age

The Greek verb Paul uses—*syschēmatizō*—means to force into a pattern. It is the language of a mold, a press, a world with its thumb upon the clay of human souls to leave its imprint upon them. And the pressure today is not gentle. It demands affirmation, not discernment. It preaches tolerance—but only of its dogmas. It punishes truth spoken plainly.

Hard Pressure: China

There are places where the mold is not subtle at all. In Communist China, the state does not merely suggest compliance—it engineers it. Unregistered house churches are raided, pastors detained, and congregations scattered. Regulations introduced over the last decade have tightened control over clergy training, banned those under eighteen from formal religious activity, and required many churches to install surveillance cameras—eyes of the state watching the pulpit.

In 2025, authorities intensified a crackdown on one of the country's prominent unregistered churches, detaining its pastor and multiple leaders on charges tied to "illegal" online ministry—part of a broader campaign to *Sinicize* the church, to press believers into a politically loyal, state-scripted faith. This is *syschēmatizō* with handcuffs—the sculptor's mold enforced by police, demanding that the Bride of Christ wear the face of the Party. The only loyalty allowed is to the state.

Soft Authoritarian Pressure: The West

But the press is not confined to overt tyrannies. In the West, it works with careful language and legal gloves. Pastors and street preachers in the U.K. and Canada have faced arrest, fines, or protracted legal battles when their public preaching on sin and salvation collided with evolving "hate speech" or "public order" laws—cases sometimes overturned, but only after the process itself declared: *this message is unwelcome here.*

In Finland, former Interior Minister and long-time parliamentarian Päivi Räsänen has spent years in court for publicly quoting Scripture and affirming historic Christian teaching—acquitted twice, yet pursued again to the Supreme Court in a landmark case testing whether biblical conviction can now be treated as criminal agitation.

Even when believers are cleared, the message to pastors is unmistakable: *Stay quiet. Stay vague. Stay safe.* The mold here is not a prison cell first—it is a chilled conscience, a tamed pulpit, a shepherd who decides that Romans 1 is too expensive to read aloud.

Whether by surveillance or statute, by open chains or quiet career threats, the strategy is the same—in Beijing, Helsinki, London, Ottawa, or Washington: press the church into a shape the age approves—or punish her until she sculpts herself.

Civil Pressure: The Pandemic Test

During the COVID outbreak in 2020, pastors in Canada and the United States faced jail time or fines for keeping their churches open without state-approved restrictions. In both nations, submission to government directives often overrode constitutional or charter guarantees of free worship.

In the United States, compliance frequently trumped the First Amendment—

> "Congress shall make no law respecting an establishment of religion, or prohibiting the free exercise thereof; or abridging the freedom of speech, or of the press; or the right of the people peaceably to assemble, and to petition the Government for a redress of grievances."

These words protect the freedoms of religion, speech, press, assembly, and petition. Yet many pastors complied, some under duress, others from misplaced deference. Moments like this do not simply test policies — they test principles and resolve. Conformity is not exposed by public debates first, but by private assumptions no longer governed by Scripture. To some observers, it felt like a beta test of pastoral obedience—an experiment in how quickly pulpits would yield to pressure.

President Andrew Jackson, in his 1837 Farewell Address, warned: *"Eternal vigilance by the people is the price of liberty."* He echoed an older truth voiced by Irish statesman John Curran in 1790: *"The condition upon which God hath given liberty to man is eternal vigilance."*

Curran's phrasing is the truer theology—liberty linked to God. If our freedom comes from God, then we are its stewards, accountable for preserving what He has entrusted. Yet we are watching those hard-won and costly freedoms erode before our eyes, too often without raising our voices.

The world rewards compromise disguised as kindness. Long before persecution becomes visible, conformity becomes normal. Do not underestimate the power of the world systems. The culture is forming us; the world is disciplining always. If the church does not shape saints, the world will shape consumers.

Spiritual *transformation* (*metamorphoō*) is not cosmetic; it is cruciform—taking the shape of the cross, mind renewed through truth, not trend.

Many pulpits feel that pressure like a vise on the conscience—soften here, qualify there, smile when you should warn, entertain when you should equip, applaud the flesh and call it grace. Like a boa constrictor, once it has its prey in its coils, continual pressure is maintained. Every time the prey exhales, the coils tighten until the life is squeezed out and the prey devoured.

Slowly, without malice or intention, a pastor lays down the shepherd's rod for the influencer's wink. But the Good Shepherd did not wink at wolves; He named them, faced them, and stood the line. So must we.

A. Political Pressure — Ideology Over Kingdom

A century of cultural strategy (from Gramsci forward) has aimed not at armies but at institutions—to replace transcendence with ideology and re-baptize power as moral authority. The result is a demand that the pulpit preach activism instead of repentance and policy instead of Kingdom.

Scripture Armory

- *"We must obey God rather than men."* (Acts 5:29)
- *"The nations rage... He who sits in the heavens laughs."* (Psalm 2)
- *"My kingdom is not of this world."* (John 18:36)

Pastoral Stance: Name Christ as King, not Caesar as savior.

B. Sociological Pressure — Group Identity Over Personal Responsibility

The script shifts: persons are reframed as victims or oppressors. Sin becomes a demographic; repentance becomes re-education. Family authority bends beneath state and school; motherhood and fatherhood are mocked or erased.

Scripture Armory

- *"Each of us will give an account of himself to God."* (Romans 14:12)

- *"God shows no partiality."* (Acts 10:34)
- *"If anyone is in Christ, he is a new creation."* (2 Corinthians 5:17)

Pastoral Stance: Preach personal repentance, personal conversion.

C. Philosophical Pressure — Truth Unmoored

Postmodern heirs (Nietzsche, Foucault, Derrida) exchanged revelation for construction: truth is power, language is oppression, meaning is fluid. Feelings outrank facts; lived experience outranks Scripture.

Scripture Armory
- *"Sanctify them in the truth; Your word is truth."* (John 17:17)
- *"The word of our God stands forever."* (Isaiah 40:8)
- *"Everyone who is of the truth listens to My voice."* (John 18:37)

Pastoral Stance: Preach objective truth without apology.

D. Economic Pressure — Consumerism & Technocracy

With truth dethroned, materialism fills the vacuum: man as consumer, church as vendor, pastor as CEO. Success is counted in budgets, buildings, and brand reach.

Scripture Armory
- *"You cannot serve God and Mammon."* (Matt. 6:24)
- *"One's life does not consist in the abundance of possessions."* (Luke 12:15)
- *"Seek first His kingdom and His righteousness."* (Matt. 6:33)

Pastoral Stance: Form stewards and saints, not consumers and spectators.

E. Moral Pressure — New Virtues, New Sins

The age canonizes affirmation and exiles holiness. The new sins are certainty, moral clarity, motherhood as calling, masculinity under mastery, and the exclusive claims of Christ. It demands we bless what God forbids and mute what God commands.

Scripture Armory
- *"Woe to those who call evil good and good evil."* (Isaiah 5:20)
- *"Be holy, for I am holy."* (1 Peter 1:16)
- *"Preach the word… in season and out of season."* (2 Timothy 4:2)

Pastoral Stance: Teach biblical virtue—without flinching.

F. Sexual & Gender Pressure — Creational Order Assaulted

Sex severed from covenant; gender severed from biology; children sexualized; marriage destabilized; image-bearers reduced to impulses; transhumanism rises to "improve" the imago Dei.

Scripture Armory
- *"Male and female He created them."* (Genesis 1:27)
- *"Marriage is to be held in honor among all."* (Hebrews 13:4)
- *Romans 1:24–27 — the exchange that deforms desire.*

Pastoral Stance: Guard marriage, manhood, womanhood, and children.

G. Technological & Information Pressure — Attention Colonized

Screens capture the mind faster than sermons. Coding curates loves and fears. The average believer is taught by feeds, not by the faith.

Scripture Armory

- *"Be transformed by the renewing of your mind."* (Romans 12:2)
- *"Set your mind on things above."* (Colossians 3:2)

"Take every thought captive to obey Christ." (2 Corinthians 10:5)

Pastoral Stance: Fight the world's mold with intentional formation.

The Enemy's Endgame

This isn't random drift; it is the slow design of de-creation:
>Unmake truth.
>Unmake identity.
>Unmake family.
>Unmake meaning.
>Unmake morality.
>Unmake worship.
>Unmake man.

All of it so that man kneels not before Christ's throne, but before the throne of the self—or the state that pledges to protect that self. This is not just culture; it is collision of kingdoms. And into that collision walks the shepherd of God.

What Happens When Pastors Yield?

Slowly, subtly, without malice:

- The rod becomes a microphone.

- The staff becomes a brand.
- The sermon becomes sentiment.
- The church becomes an audience.
- The pastor becomes an influencer.
- The Bible becomes a suggestion.
- And the flock becomes prey.

So we tone-check truth. Soften here. Qualify there. Apologize for Scripture. Smile when you should warn. Entertain where you should equip. Applaud the flesh and call it grace. Little by little, the shepherd's rod is traded for the influencer's wink.

Not on our watch.

Called to Stand Apart
"Do not be conformed to this world." Not suggestion—command. Not retreat from mission—but refusal to assimilate. This world system—its thinking, its values, its idols—is passing away. To blend with it is to lash your boat to a sinking ship.

We do not mirror the world; we magnify Christ. We do not borrow identity from tribe or party; we are crucified with Christ and raised to a new nature. Identity politics fractures; Christ unites. Activism burns out; the gospel transforms. Trend-chasing exhausts; truth anchors.

Daniel stood when all bowed. Esther spoke when silence was safer. Peter and John answered, *"We must obey God rather than men."* (Acts 5:29) They did not stand defiant; they stood obedient. Holiness is not stubbornness—it is allegiance.

Transformed by Renewal
Conformity is easy; transformation is cruciform. God does not give His people spiritual cosmetics; He gives resurrection life. Renewing the mind is not positive thinking; it is Scripture saturat-

ing, Spirit teaching, Christ shaping the inner man until the outer life bears the imprint of heaven, not Hollywood; Zion, not Wall Street; Kingdom, not D.C.

Our greatest enemy is not merely immoral culture—it is unrenewed minds in the pew and unguarded pulpits in the land. Entertainment replaced edification. Therapy eclipsed theology. Sermons became sentiment with a verse stapled to the end. But Christ did not bleed to form a comfort club. He died and rose to form a holy nation.

Churches don't need more stage lights; they need renewed minds. They don't need more personalities; they need purity. They don't need better branding; they need better bracing—steel in the spine, Scripture in the bones, Spirit in the breath.

The Jesus Who Will Not Fit in a Soft Pulpit

There is a crisis in modern preaching: we have painted Jesus in pastels when Scripture reveals Him in fire. We whisper comfort where He issues commands. We present a divine therapist rather than the conquering King. Correct the record.

The Christ who saves is the Christ who shakes. Preach Him full, not half—the Shepherd and the Warrior, the cross and the crown, the thorns and the throne.

Not Meek and Mild—But Mighty and Majestic

"Do not think I came to bring peace, but a sword." (Matt. 10:34) A sword divides, confronts, demands a choice. He did not allow darkness; He scattered it. Where He walked, hell panicked.

The Jesus Who Confronts Demons

The Gadarenes heard the shriek: *"What have You to do with us?"* He didn't counsel spirits; He commanded them: *"Come out of him!"* (Mark 5:8) Chains snapped. A tombed-man sat clothed and sane. Devils fled like smoke before a storm wind.

The Jesus Who Storms Gates
"I will build My church, and the gates of hell shall not prevail against it." (Matthew 16:18) Gates don't attack; they resist attack. Hell is on defense, not offense. Christ didn't form a monastery—He formed an army.

The Jesus Who Cleansed the Temple
He braided a whip—judgment wound strand by strand. Tables upended, coins scattering, men running. No listening session with money-changers. No "Temple Reform Roundtable." Holiness drove corruption out. Pastors who tremble to confront compromise do not look like their Master; they look like His accusers.

The Christ Soldiers Saluted
Hardened Roman centurions recognized true command. During His ministry, a centurion came to Jesus to request that He heal his servant. Jesus offered to go to the centurion's house. The soldier recognized the authority of Jesus: *"Only say the word, and my servant will be healed."* (Matthew 8:8)

At the cross, another centurion saw it under fire—watching how Jesus suffered, how He yielded His spirit, how creation itself responded—and declared, *"Truly this man was the Son of God"* (Matthew 27:54; Mark 15:39; Luke 23:47). This was not sentimentality. It was recognition.

Hardened men trained to obey power do not kneel to weakness. They kneel to authority. Even in death, Christ did not lose command—He revealed it. The centurion's confession was, in its own way, a soldier's salute.

This is the Christ who orders angels as easily as breathing, who allowed nails only because love demanded sacrifice.

Each centurion moment serves a distinct role (distance, suffering, death). Soldiers respond to command presence, authority.

No soldier bows to frailty; they bow to a King.

Son of David—Shepherd and Warrior
The Messiah is not only Son of God—He is Son of David: harp and sling, psalms and sword. David learned courage in the fields. A lion came—he struck it. A bear rose—he killed it. A giant advanced—he ran toward him. He didn't grab a sling for the first time that day; he had trained in obscurity for victory in daylight.

Why five stones? Because Goliath had four brothers. Readiness is not luck; it is faith with foresight. Six hundred mighty men would have died for him—not because he was tender alone, but because he was fearless and righteous. Saul has slain his thousands; David his ten-thousands. A shepherd who could sing over lambs and break wolves' jaws with a sling.

This is the lineage of Jesus. He is the Good Shepherd—tender and true. He is the Warrior-King—victorious and unyielding. Pastor, to reflect Him, you must be both. Carry the staff and the rod. Speak comfort and truth. Sing to the weary and stand against the wolves. Do not apologize for strength. Do not blush at authority. Do not declaw the gospel.

Refuse the Mold
Pastor—hear this as from a brother in the trench: the hour demands courage more than polish. You are not a cruise director; you are a watchman.

Feed them Scripture.
Form them in Christ.
Train them for obedience.
Teach them to discern.
Guard them from wolves.
Model holiness...And when necessary—bleed for them.

Kindness is not cowardice. Gentleness is not abdication. Love tells the truth even when it stings. Refuse the mold of the celebrity pastor. Refuse the mold of the culture-pleaser. Refuse the mold that defines success as applause and peace as silence. Choose faithfulness over fame; holiness over hype; and truth over trend.

A New Humanity Rising

The church is not a brand; she is a bride. Not a content platform; a consecrated people. Not a moral minority; a royal priesthood, an embassy of another Kingdom. When the world presses—we show another pattern. When the earth shakes—we stand unshaken. When culture calls for compromise—we answer with conviction. This is not stubborn nostalgia; it is Spirit-born identity.

We are citizens of a Kingdom that cannot be shaken (Hebrews 12:28). We are members of a body the gates of hell cannot overcome (Matthew 16:18). We are children of a Father who does not negotiate truth (Numbers 23:19).

The world molds masses. Christ forms men and women who shine like steel in the cold dawn—forged, tempered, ready.

A Holy Hush — Behold the Christ We Preach

Pastor, before you lift your voice, lift your eyes. Behold Christ of Patmos vision and Gethsemane grit—robe dipped in blood, voice like many waters, feet like burnished bronze, gaze that searches nations and men (Rev. 1; 19). Let awe settle like snow on ancient pines. You serve no small King. You preach no soft Master. You carry no mild gospel. Let the hush do its holy work.

A Holy Fire — Courage Rises

The Christ who wept over Jerusalem braided a whip and cleansed His Father's house. The Christ who carried lambs crushed the serpent's head. The Christ who forgave from the cross will break the nations with a rod of iron. You stand in David's line—harp in one hand, sling in the other; psalm on the lips, steel in the soul. The oil on your head is not decorative—it is war paint. You are not sent to cushion sheep into comfort but to form them into saints who can stand. Let fire burn in your bones again.

A Holy Resolve — We Will Not Bend

Rise—slow, steady, certain. The world presses. We do not yield. Hell fortifies. We advance. Giants roar. We run toward them. Culture shouts its counterfeit gospel. We preach Christ crucified and risen—King and Commander, Shepherd and Sovereign, Lamb and Lion.

The world calls for timidity. We answer with truth. The age demands compromise. We answer with conviction. And when wolves come—as they will—you will not flinch. Staff in hand. Rod at your side. Sling ready. Heart steady. Eyes on Christ. We march under the banner of the Warrior-King. And victory is sure.

Benediction for Lion-Hearted Shepherds

Lord Jesus, Captain of our salvation, King of glory, Shepherd of souls—

Grant Your servants awe before Your throne, fire in their bones, and steel in their spines.

Raise up shepherds who will stand. Make them gentle with the broken, fierce against the devourer.

Give them a heart like David's, courage like Daniel's, clarity like Paul's, and fidelity like the prophets who would not bow.

Let their pulpits burn with Scripture, their prayers rattle darkness, their lives bear the marks of obedience, and their churches become embassies of Your Kingdom. Amen.

5

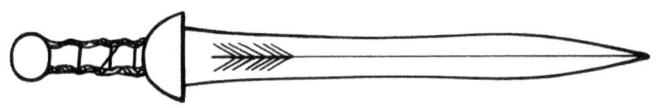

Reclaiming the Real Church

Christ Among the Lampstands

Christ walks among His churches. Not as a distant observer or a symbolic presence, but as the living Lord who still examines His people and weighs their faithfulness. *"Then I turned to see the voice that spoke with me… and in the midst of the lampstands One like the Son of Man"* (Revelation 1:12–13). Before He ever addressed empires or rulers, He addressed congregations — gathered bodies in real places, with real names, real strengths, and real sins.

The seven churches of Asia form a mirror and a warning for the modern church. They show us how faith communities, in any era, can either hold the line or lose it.

We can draw from *Revelation 2–3* **a diagnostic for every generation of the church** — a kind of spiritual MRI showing how health turns to sickness and what renewal looks like. If Romans 12:2 warns us not to be molded, Revelation 2–3 shows us what happens when we are—and how Christ calls His churches back.

Lessons from the Seven Churches of Asia
1. Ephesus – Orthodoxy Without Affection
"You have persevered and have endured hardships for my name, and have not grown weary. Yet I hold this against you: You have forsaken the love you had at first." (Revelation 2:3–4)

Ephesus had correct doctrine and strong endurance — everything a healthy church should. But it had lost its affection for Christ.

<u>The danger</u>: **Truth without love becomes hardness.**

<u>The lesson for us</u>: In standing against the culture, we must not forget the heart that fuels obedience. A church that loses its first love soon becomes a museum of its former faith. When the light of first love dims, another philosophy always moves in to claim the vacant altar.

Montana Plain: "You can polish a plow till it shines, but if it's not turning soil, it's just a decoration."

2. Smyrna – Faithful Amid Suffering
"I know your afflictions and your poverty—yet you are rich." (Revelation 2:9)

Smyrna was small, poor, and persecuted — but pure. They had no rebuke, only encouragement.

<u>The danger</u>: None — only endurance.

<u>The lesson</u>: Faithfulness under fire is the seed of future revival. The church doesn't need power to prevail; it needs purity.

Montana Plain: "You don't know how strong your roots are till the storm hits."

3. Pergamum – Compromise in the Shadow of Power
"You live where Satan has his throne. Yet you remain true to my name... Nevertheless, you have people there who hold to the teaching of Balaam." (Revelation 2:13–14)

Pergamum stood in the heart of idolatry and political influence — and some compromised to survive.

The danger: **Accommodation.** The church that seeks the favor of Caesar always loses the favor of Christ.

The lesson: Standing near power is not the same as standing in truth.

Montana Plain: "Once you start trimming your message to fit the audience, it's not the Gospel anymore — it's advertising."

4. Thyatira – Tolerance as a Virtue

"You tolerate that woman Jezebel, who calls herself a prophet." (Revelation 2:20)

Thyatira's sin was moral tolerance dressed as compassion. They allowed false teaching to masquerade as mercy.

The danger: **Corruption of conscience.**

The lesson: Every age that worships tolerance eventually reaps tyranny. The church must distinguish between love for sinners and approval of sin.

Montana Plain: "Mercy without truth isn't mercy—it's malpractice."

5. Sardis – Reputation Without Reality

"You have a reputation of being alive, but you are dead." (Revelation. 3:1)

Sardis looked alive — busy, active, well-branded — but spiritually lifeless.

The danger: **Image replacing substance.**

The lesson: It's possible to have motion without mission, activity without anointing. Revival begins when the church admits that the lights are on but nobody's home.

6. Philadelphia – Little Strength, Great Faith

"You have little strength, yet you have kept my word and have not denied my name." (Revelation 3:8)

Philadelphia wasn't large or powerful, but it was faithful. Christ promised to open a door no one could shut.

The danger: None — but a call to endurance.

The lesson: God delights to use small, faithful churches to shame the proud. The remnant doesn't need a crowd — only conviction.

Montana Plain: "God can do more with a handful of wheat than a barn full of chaff."

7. Laodicea – Lukewarm Luxury

"You say, 'I am rich; I have acquired wealth and do not need a thing.' But you do not realize that you are wretched, pitiful, poor, blind and naked." (Revelation 3:17)

Laodicea is the final stage of spiritual captivity — comfort mistaken for blessing. They were self-sufficient, self-satisfied, and spiritually blind.

The danger: **Apathy and self-deception.**

The lesson: A lukewarm church is one sip away from being spat out. God's remedy is not adjustment but repentance.

Montana Plain: "You can't warm your hands at yesterday's fire."

The Composite Picture

If we chart the seven, we get a diagnosis that has parallels in our own era:

Church	Disease	Modern Parallel
Ephesus	Lost love	Orthodoxy without passion
Smyrna	Suffering	The persecuted remnant
Pergamum	Compromise	The politically entangled church
Thyatira	Tolerance	The progressive, affirming church
Sardis	Reputation	The consumer-driven mega-church
Philadelphia	Faithful remnant	Small but steadfast believers
Laodicea	Lukewarm comfort	The affluent, complacent church

The seven profiles give us a composite picture of the church's vulnerabilities in every age.

- Ephesus reveals orthodoxy without affection—truth with a cooling heart.
- Smyrna displays costly faithfulness—the persecuted remnant, rich in what heaven counts.
- Pergamum exposes compromise in the shadow of power—the church that wants both Christ and Caesar's smile.
- Thyatira embodies tolerance gone toxic—confusing approval of sin with love for sinners.
- Sardis stands as reputation without reality—a church busy, branded, and spiritually asleep.
- Philadelphia shines as the faithful remnant—little strength, open doors, steady obedience.
- Laodicea chills the soul as lukewarm luxury—wealthy, self-assured, blind to its own poverty.

Together they trace the path from fire to form, from devotion to drift. And they hint at the way back: a return to the spirit of Philadelphia—faithfulness over fame, conviction over convenience.

These seven letters become the **spiritual backdrop**. They show the same story we've been tracing:
- **Collapse (Laodicea and Sardis)**
- **Remnant (Philadelphia and Smyrna)**
- **Correction and Call to Stand (Ephesus, Pergamum, Thyatira)**

Ephesus and Smyrna, Pergamum and Thyatira, Sardis and Philadelphia and Laodicea: seven lampstands, seven conditions of the soul, seven portraits that have mirrored God's people in every age. And in our time, if you listen with the ears of the Spirit and look with clear eyes, you can still see each of them. Some congregations burn bright with devotion and endurance. Others shine with polish but are hollow as an empty drum. Some cling to reputation; others cling to Christ.

Each church is a snapshot of a modern condition, each a call to stand in its own way in the current culture. The pattern is sobering: from fire to form, from love to lukewarm, from witness to comfort—unless we return to the Philadelphian spirit, where faithfulness outranks fame and conviction outruns convenience.

The Lord has not changed, nor has His church ceased to be a field hospital and an outpost of the Kingdom. But the question He asked then is the question He asks now: *What kind of church have we become?*

Stand and see. Christ still inspects His ranks.

The Church as Christ's Continuing Presence

For the church is not an idea. It is not a brand, a franchise strategy, a broadcast center, or a production environment. It is the incarnate presence of Christ in the world — His body, His witness, His lamp in the valley of the shadow. *"For by one Spirit we were all baptized into one body" (1 Corinthians 12:13).*

The Incarnation did not end when Jesus ascended; it multiplied. What He once embodied in one frame, He now indwells in many. *"Now you are the body of Christ, and members individually"* (1 Corinthians 12:27). And when a local assembly gathers in His name and walks in His ways, heaven touches earth in that place.

When a church trades reverence for relevance, proclamation for performance, or Spirit-powered discipleship for consumer-satisfying programming, light fades and the lampstand trembles.

Christ does not inhabit marketing plans — only surrendered hearts.

The Lampstands and the Local Church

When Jesus dictated letters to the seven churches of Asia, He didn't address a single bishop, council, or papal seat. He spoke directly to congregations — **Ephesus, Smyrna, Pergamum, Thyatira, Sardis, Philadelphia, Laodicea** — each with its own identity, virtues, and failures. These were independent assemblies, yet each was a *lampstand* in His hand (Revelation 1:20).

In the New Testament, the church is never portrayed as a top-down institution. Leadership was plural and local — elders, deacons, shepherds — all accountable to Christ as the head. The pattern is consistent from Jerusalem to Antioch to Philippi and Corinth. Paul writes *"To the church of God that is in Corinth,"* not *"to the diocese of Achaia."*

The Congregational Principle

Every local church is a full expression of the Body of Christ. It has the same Lord, the same Spirit, the same mission. That's why the letters to the seven churches still speak to us: they are **timeless diagnostics** for any congregation in any century.

Hierarchical systems — Episcopal, Methodist, Lutheran — tend to move as whole bodies; their decisions ripple downward. But in the New Testament pattern, **responsibility is distributed**, not centralized. Each congregation stands or falls by its own obedience. Christ walks among the lampstands, examining each one individually.

Montana Plain: "Jesus doesn't send memos to headquarters — He knocks on local doors."

The Choice Before Every Church

The modern church in America mirrors this tension. Some have chosen the path of Ephesus — sound in doctrine but cold in love. Others drift like Pergamum, cozy with political power. Some, like Sardis, live off the reputation of past vitality. And scattered among them are Philadelphian congregations — small, faithful, holding fast to the Word.

The question isn't which age of church history we're in; it's **which type of church we've become**.

- Will we trade conviction for comfort?
- Will we measure success by numbers or by faithfulness?
- Will we wait for national revival while neglecting the one thing within our reach — revival in our own fellowship?

The Local Stand

Revelation ends its letters with seven personal appeals: *"He who has an ear, let him hear."* Every church, and every believer within it, must decide whether to heed that call. The remnant begins not with a movement but with a congregation — one that still believes Christ walks among the lampstands and still burns to shine.

Montana Plain: "If the whole valley goes dark, one steady lantern still keeps the night honest."

The Seven Churches in Our Time
Ephesus with its orthodoxy and waning affection — *"You have left your first love"* (Revelation 2:4).
Smyrna with its scars and steadfastness — *"Be faithful unto death"* (Revelation 2:10).
Pergamum negotiating with power — *"You hold fast My name... but you have those who hold false teaching"* (Rev. 2:13–14).
Thyatira confusing false mercy with love — *"You tolerate Jezebel"* (Revelation 2:20).
Sardis polishing reputation while the Spirit departs — *"You have a name that you are alive, but you are dead"* (Revelation 3:1).
Philadelphia holding fast — *"You have little strength, but have kept My word"* (Revelation 3:8).
Laodicea wealthy and blind — *"You say 'I am rich'... but you are naked"* (Revelation 3:17).

We do not need to ask which era we live in; we need to ask which church we have become. **Revival begins when diagnosis becomes repentance.** But light resisted is light opposed—and in the last century that opposition learned new tactics.

From Lampstands to the Long March
If the church is Christ's living presence in the world, then she is also the principal impediment to any creed that seeks to dethrone God and enthrone man. Lampstands don't merely illuminate; they expose. A people indwelt by the Spirit, preaching a crucified and

risen Lord, unmask the lie at the heart of every utopia: that man can save himself if only the right engineers hold the levers. *"For the weapons of our warfare are not of the flesh, but mighty before God to the tearing down of strongholds"* (2 Corinthians 10:4).

Antonio Gramsci understood this better than many pastors. He saw that Western strength did not rest first in parliaments or police, but in pulpits, prayer, family tables, and catechized consciences. If Marxism was to advance, the church could not simply be ignored; she had to be captured, neutralized, or shamed into silence. The battlefield would be imagination and vocabulary, not barricades and bayonets. Change the meanings of words, and you change the memory of a people. Change the memory, and you can redirect their worship.

After the upheavals of the 1960s, the opportunity arrived. Exhausted by cultural conflict and enticed by the promise of relevance, many congregations began to trade proclamation for peace treaties with the age. The Frankfurt School supplied the grammar; the spirit of the times supplied the appetite. Gradually, pulpits learned to speak the dialect of self, therapies replaced repentance, technique eclipsed truth. The sentry laid down his trumpet because applause felt kinder than alarm. *"Contend earnestly for the faith which was once for all delivered to the saints"* (Jude 3) became, in practice, *"Avoid offense at any cost."*

This is how the line was turned—quietly, locally, respectably. Not by outlawing the church, but by outfitting her with the culture's armor and telling her it was love. The lampstand still stood in many places, but the oil grew thin. And with the light dimmed, the long march quickened its pace.

Montana Plain: "If you hand your post to the passerby, don't be surprised when he changes the orders."

How the Church Was Captured

1. The Slow Exchange — From Revelation to Relevance

The first breach was not in doctrine but in *desire*. As culture shifted from truth to preference, the church wanted to be loved more than to be listened to.

In the mid-20th century, pastors began trading the pulpit's prophetic stance for the platform of respectability. The question changed from *"Is it true?"* to *"Will they like it?"*

By the time the Jesus Movement reached the suburbs, the vocabulary of "felt needs" and "relevance" had replaced "repentance" and "holiness." The church forgot that friendship with the world has always been purchased with silence.

Montana Plain: "You can't be salt if you're worried about being sugar."

2. The Intellectual Breach — Liberal Theology and the Loss of the Supernatural

The second breach came through the seminaries. By the early 1900s, German higher criticism had crossed the Atlantic. It taught future ministers to doubt the reliability of Scripture while claiming to defend it "scientifically." Miracles were reinterpreted as myths, sin as maladjustment, and salvation as self-realization.

This academic softening hollowed out entire denominations. Churches still used the same words — *grace, faith, resurrection* — but the dictionary had changed. When the intellect dethrones revelation, the pulpit becomes an echo chamber of culture.

3. The Cultural Capture — Consumerism in the Sanctuary

After World War II, America's economic boom birthed the **Church-Growth Movement**. The business model of Madison Avenue replaced the shepherd model of Acts. Success was measured in attendance, not obedience; budgets, not brokenness.

The sanctuary adopted the logic of the shopping mall: give the people what they want, and they'll keep coming back. Music became marketing. Programs became products. The congregation became a customer base.

Montana Plain: "When the sheep start rating the shepherd by the buffet, it's only a matter of time before wolves open a franchise."

4. The Moral Drift — Sexual Revolution and the Redefinition of Sin

The 1960s and 70s tore up the moral floorboards. Many churches mistook compassion for compromise, believing that to love people meant to approve their choices. The vocabulary of holiness was slowly replaced with the language of therapy.

Sin became "brokenness." Conviction became *judgmentalism*. This drift didn't merely weaken moral clarity; it rewired conscience. When the church refused to name sin, the culture renamed it virtue.

5. The Ideological Infiltration — Marxist Categories in Christian Clothes

By the 1980s and 90s, the ideas sown by Gramsci and the Frankfurt School were flowering in universities — and the church began hiring their graduates.

Critical theory's categories of *oppressor vs. oppressed* slipped into sermons. Justice was redefined without reference to holiness; liberation was preached without repentance.

Pastors began quoting activists more than apostles. The pulpit adopted the language of grievance instead of grace. Under the banner of compassion, a new orthodoxy took root — one that judged truth by emotion and morality by power.

6. The Digital Distraction — Noise as the New Silence

The modern church now swims in constant information but with little formation. We are well-informed but under-trained. We hear sermons, consume podcasts, and scroll endless content, yet too few believers are being shaped in character, conviction, and courage. We consume truth but are not being changed by it.

Screens glow where altars once stood. People scroll through sermons as they do songs — two minutes in, swipe to the next.

The Word competes with algorithms trained to keep attention short and affections shallow. It's hard to hear the still small voice when you're always wearing earbuds.

7. The Final Stage — Self at the Center

It ends where the serpent began: *"You will be like God."* The church's captivity is complete when faith becomes self-help, worship becomes performance, and theology becomes mere myth.

We no longer ask, "What is God's will?" but "What does this mean for me?"

This is the final inversion — when the Bride starts courting her reflection instead of her Bridegroom.

The Pattern Behind It All

If you chart the sequence, the degradation looks like this:

Stage	Substitution	Result
Revelation	→ Relevance	Loss of authority
Doctrine	→ Doubt	Loss of confidence
Shepherding	→ Marketing	Loss of authenticity
Holiness	→ Therapy	Loss of conviction
Gospel	→ Ideology	Loss of clarity
Worship	→ Entertainment	Loss of presence
God	→ Self	Loss of soul

The slide always follows the same path: revelation is traded for relevance, and authority is lost. Doctrine is replaced by doubt, and confidence is lost. Shepherding yields to marketing, and authenticity is lost. Holiness is absorbed into therapy, and conviction is lost. The gospel is bent into ideology, and clarity is lost. Worship turns into entertainment, and the sense of presence is lost. In the end, God is quietly replaced by the self—and the soul is lost.

When the Sanctuary Began to Echo the World

Somewhere along the way, much of the American church forgot what it was meant to be. Not all — thank God for the faithful. But many found themselves seduced by the language of technique and success. A generation ago, Norman Vincent Peale stood in New York preaching a gospel of positive thinking — hope without holiness, affirmation without repentance.

In California, Robert Schuller built a cathedral of glass and optimism, offering encouragement while quietly removing the offense of the cross. Later came the era of the seeker-sensitive sanctuary, perfected at Willow Creek: a church designed to attract the curious, entertain the unchurched, and avoid any word that might sound like surrender or sin. And it worked — in the short term. Crowds came. Buildings expanded. Media praised the model. Conferences multiplied.

Until the fruit was tested. And it was found light. *"Having a form of godliness but denying its power"* (2 Timothy 3:5).

When the sanctuary mirrors the world, the world never meets Christ.

The Seeker Church Confession

Willow Creek confessed what discernment already knew: crowds do not equal disciples. You can build an audience and starve a flock. You can fill rows and empty souls.

When the survey results arrived, they discovered what Jesus warned all along — sheep cannot live on cotton candy. Churches were full, but believers were thin. Worshippers attended, but few could feed themselves on the Word.

The founder fell; the movement faltered under the weight of its own success. Numbers had become the idol. The sanctuary had become a stage. And all the while, the lampstand flickered. *"Remember therefore from where you have fallen; repent and do the first works"* (Revelation 2:5).

God does not reward attendance — He rewards obedience.

Why It Happened

That did not happen accidentally. It was not simply misguided zeal. It happened because the church, in its insecurity, began taking cues from the world it was called to confront.

Marketing language replaced apostolic language. Relevance eclipsed reverence; psychology borrowed the pulpit. And the Gospel was translated into therapeutic slogans. The cross became a symbol of comfort rather than the instrument of death that leads to life. *"If anyone would come after Me, let him deny himself, take up his cross daily, and follow Me"* (Luke 9:23).

And slowly, without riots or revolutions, the sanctuary became an annex of the culture rather than a witness against it.

The Church does not lose battles — it forfeits them.

Christ Still Walks the Line

But Christ still walks His line. He walks into small mountain chapels and downtown sanctuaries, into rural fellowships and urban storefronts, into weathered log-churches on the plains and brick steeples in old American towns. He knows where the fire burns clean and where the embers glow only from yesterday's flame.

He hears the prayers whispered in barns and living rooms, in basements and hospital corridors, where believers gather with little strength but unshaken faith. He knows the pulpits where pastors still preach the Word plainly and pray like heaven listens. And He sees the sanctuaries where fog machines roll, lights flash, and souls leave unfed though the room was full.

The seven churches stand before us still — each one alive and visible. Some shining. Some smoldering. Some hollow but loud. Some quiet but faithful. Christ sees them all.

The eyes of fire still search the house of God (Rev. 1:14).

If capture came by slow exchange, recovery will come by holy reversal.

The Way Back: Returning, Not Innovating

Reclaiming the real church is not a strategy; it is a return. It is the remembrance of the first love, the recovery of holiness, the restoration of prayer, the re-centering of preaching, the reawakening of conscience, and the refusal to measure success by applause, metrics, or cultural favor. We measure ourselves by the standard of the Pentecost church: *42And they devoted themselves to the apostles' teaching and the fellowship, to the breaking of bread and the prayers. 43And awe came upon every soul, and many wonders and signs were being done through the apostles. 44And all who believed were together and had all things in common. 45And they were selling their possessions and belongings and distributing the proceeds to all, as any had need. 46And day by day, attending the temple together and breaking bread in their homes, they received their food with glad and generous hearts,*

47praising God and having favor with all the people. And the Lord added to their number day by day those who were being saved (Acts 2:42-47).

It is Christ in the midst again — not as a concept, but as a commanding presence. It is pastors treating their pulpits as command posts, not performance stages. It is congregations choosing obedience over optics, depth over draw, faithfulness over fashion.

It is the recovery of courage, the renewal of reverence, the rebuilding of spiritual stamina, and the refusal to surrender the sanctuary to the spirit of the age.

Revival will not come through innovation — but through consecration.

When the Commander Inspects His Ranks

When Christ walks among His lampstands today, let Him find us awake. Let Him hear prayers rising like incense, not slogans flashing like roadside diner signs. Let Him find disciples, not spectators; soldiers, not consumers.

Let Him find pastors who shepherd instead of brand, saints who worship instead of watch, and churches that send rather than simply provide cushy seats. Let Him find Philadelphia faith in Laodicean times.

His intent is loving correction, not mere critique: *"Those whom I love, I reprove and discipline; therefore be zealous and repent* (Revelation 3:19)."

The remnant does not rise with a roar but with a resolve. It begins not in cathedrals but in humble sanctuaries and quiet living rooms where saints bow their heads, open their Bibles, and say, "Lord, make us faithful again."

The Lord does not seek crowds — He seeks courage.

The Church That Remembers Her Calling

It is a return to that first room after the Ascension, where ordinary believers waited in prayer and power fell like wind and flame. When the church remembers who she is — the indwelt body of the risen Christ, sent into the world as light into darkness — she becomes dangerous again.

Not angry, but anchored. Not loud, but luminous. Not fashionable, but faithful. A church that stays in the barn too long forgets how to plow. But those who harness themselves to Christ and set their hands to the field will see harvest again — not because of numbers, but because of obedience.

The lampstands are being examined once more. The Commander of the Armies of Heaven still walks among His ranks. And those who stand, who love, who guard their doctrine and kindle their devotion, will find that Christ does not abandon His church. He purifies it. He strengthens it. He sends it.

And the night is never too dark for one steady lantern to be the beacon home.

The Spirit and the Bride say: Stand.

God's Standard

The measure of a Spirit-filled church is not found in its walls but in its witness. The Spirit who indwells us also sends us. From the first upper room to the farthest frontier, the pattern has not changed — the gathered church becomes the scattered church. As Jesus said, *"You shall receive power when the Holy Spirit has come upon you, and you shall be My witnesses"* (Acts 1:8).

The command to "make disciples" in the Great Commission is not a call to special missionaries. It is the daily rhythm of disciples who carry the presence of Christ into their ordinary worlds.

The word that appears as the command, "Go" in most of our English translations is actually a participial phrase that tells us how we are to be making disciples. A better translation is *"As we are going"* — meaning that as we are going about our daily lives—teaching, working, raising families, serving neighbors — we are proclaiming the Good News: that humanity's rebellion met God's mercy at the cross, that forgiveness is full, final, free, and forever, and that new life is available to all who believe.

When the church remembers this, worship becomes fuel for witness, fellowship becomes preparation for faithfulness, discipleship equips ministers of common life, and every congregation becomes an outpost of the Kingdom. The remnant that will rise is not defined by size or status but by obedience — a people indwelt, empowered, and sent.

But you are a chosen race, a royal priesthood, a holy nation, a people for his own possession, that you may proclaim the excellencies of him who called you out of darkness into his marvelous light.

1 Peter 2:9 ESV

6

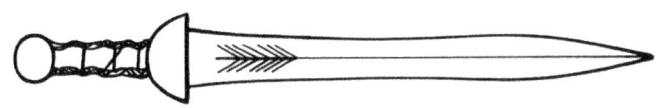

The Priesthood of All Believers

The quiet crisis in the modern church is not a lack of passion, programs, or personnel. It is a misunderstanding of who the church actually is. Over time, we have narrowed ministry to a few and reduced the many to spectators. We have trained people to attend, consume, and applaud—but not to carry Christ into the world as His sent ones.

This was not the design. From the beginning, God did not intend His people to be served by a religious class while the rest watched. He formed a people—a living body—indwelt by His Spirit, equipped by His word and grace gifts, and deployed into daily life as witnesses. Leadership existed not to replace the ministry of the saints, but to equip it. When that pattern is lost, the church does not merely become inefficient; it becomes fragile.

Recovering the priesthood of all believers is not a strategy for church growth. It is a return to biblical identity. It dismantles the false wall between "clergy" and "laity," restores ministry as shared vocation, and reclaims the New Testament vision of a sent, Spirit-indwelt people. What follows is not innovation—it is retrieval. Not nostalgia—but obedience.

1. The Original Design: A People, Not a Program

When the church was born, it did not look like an institution. It did not look like Rome. It did not look like a denomination. It looked like a fellowship.

From the very first days after Pentecost, believers gathered in homes and courtyards. They prayed. They broke bread. They listened to the apostles' teaching. They cared for one another's needs. They worshiped. They testified. And then they went back into their towns and families and workplaces and told people about Jesus.

There was no professional class set apart to "do ministry" for everyone else. Ministry was the shared work of the body.

This wasn't an accident. The New Testament church grew directly out of the synagogue pattern that had sustained the Jewish people through exile. When the Jews were dragged off to Babylon, the Temple was gone. The sacrifices were gone. The priesthood, for most practical purposes, was gone. But the people still had the word of God and one another. So they gathered wherever they could — in small assemblies for prayer, for Scripture, for instruction, for mutual care. That gathering was the synagogue.

The synagogue model was simple:

- The people chose elders — godly, proven men who were responsible for the spiritual and practical care of the community.
- Those elders appointed teachers to open the Scriptures.
- Needs were met inside the fellowship.

Every synagogue was independent, accountable to God, shaped by Scripture, and responsible for its own people. It wasn't a state department. It wasn't a franchise. It was a living community.

By the time of Jesus and the apostles, this pattern was familiar: a gathered people under the word of God, led by recognized elders, ordered around Scripture, prayer, and shared life. The churches of Acts are this pattern reborn in resurrection light.

The early churches took that same pattern and carried it straight forward. When Paul and Barnabas preached Christ in the cities of the Roman world, people believed — Jews, proselytes, and Gentile "God-fearers" who had already been gathering with the synagogue because they were hungry for one true God and a moral center. Out of those believing circles, new congregations formed.

Then what? Luke tells us plainly: *"They preached the gospel to that city and made many disciples. Then they returned… strengthening the souls of the disciples… and they appointed elders for them in every church, praying with fasting, they committed them to the Lord"* (Acts 14:21–23).

That one sentence is loaded. Paul did not set up branch offices reporting back to headquarters. He appointed elders — plural — in every local church. Each church had its own shepherding leadership, chosen from among the believers, prayed over, entrusted to the Lord.

Decentralized. Local. Accountable. Alive.

This wasn't improvisation—it was continuity. The church was not a departure from Israel's gathered life but its Spirit-filled fulfillment.

Montana Plain: "The early church wasn't run from an office. It was run from a table."

That is the blueprint.

2. Shepherds, Not Celebrities

Now look closely at what those early leaders were called, because this matters. In Acts 20, Paul calls for the "elders" of the church at Ephesus to meet him. When they arrive, he tells them that the Holy Spirit has made them "overseers" and charges them to "shepherd" the flock of God (Acts 20:17, 28).

Three different words—Elder (*presbyteros)*; Overseer (*episkopos*); Shepherd (*poimen*). One group of men.

We use different English words today — elder, bishop, pastor — and we tend to imagine those as different ranks. Paul did not. To him they were all the same men doing overlapping work: caring, guarding, teaching, feeding, watching over.

Peter says the same thing: "*As a fellow elder... I exhort the elders among you: shepherd God's flock that is among you, watching over them — not because you must, but because you are willing... not lording it over those entrusted to you, but being examples to the flock*" (1 Peter 5:1–3).

Again:
- Elders (*presbyteros*: older, spiritually mature leader).
- Shepherd (*poimēn* [noun]/ *poimainō* [verb]— shepherd / to shepherd, tend, feed).
- Watch over (*episkopountes*, from *episkopeō*—exercising oversight; related to episkopos, overseer/bishop)
- Not lording it. Be examples.

Those aren't titles. Those are functions. A pastor in the New Testament is not a brand. He is not the guy with better lighting. He is not the keynote speaker of a weekly show. He is a shepherd out in front, willing to get between the flock and the wolf. That's biblical leadership.

When shepherds feed themselves instead of the flock, God calls it evil (Ezekiel 34). When they flatter instead of warn, He calls them worthless watchmen (Jeremiah 23). Heaven does not recognize celebrity pastors—only faithful ones.

Ephesians 4:11–12 sharpens the job description even more: *"And He gave some to be apostles, and some prophets, and some evangelists, and some pastor-teachers, for the equipping of the saints for the work of ministry."*

According to Paul, the job of the pastor-teacher is not to do the ministry while everyone else watches. The job is to equip the saints to do the ministry. In New Testament terms, the "minister" is not the man up front. The "ministers" are the people.

Montana Plain: "If only one arm's swinging, the body just walks in circles."

That's where we went off the rails. We turned pastors into performers and turned congregations into consumers. Biblically, that is about as far from original design as you can get.

3. How We Lost It: When the Church Cloned the Empire

So if the New Testament model was local, shared, Spirit-led, and built on service... where did the machine come from? History gives us a hard answer.

For the first three centuries, churches were small, mostly house-based, and self-governing. Elders shepherded. Deacons served. The gifts of the Spirit flowed through the gathered body to meet needs, strengthen faith, and fuel witness. Each congregation was a lampstand, and Christ Himself walked among them.

But then something massive happened...Rome.

When Christianity was finally tolerated, then favored, then declared the state religion under Theodosius in A.D. 380, the church received a gift and a poison in the same cup. The gift was protection from persecution. The poison was power.

Rome did what empires always do: it organized. It imposed structure. It imposed ranks. It imposed lines of reporting. It took its own map — provinces, dioceses, vicars, overseers — and laid that map on top of the church. Bishops weren't just local shepherds anymore; they became regional administrators. Authority that used to flow from Scripture and Spirit now flowed through office and chain of command.

As Will Durant observed, Rome handed the church "a vast framework of government." The church—especially the church of Rome-- "followed in the footsteps of the Roman state; it conquered the provinces… and established discipline and unity from frontier to frontier."

Or, as Father Kevin Clinton put it bluntly: "We cloned the Roman Empire."

With empire-shaped structure came empire-shaped temptation. Because once you build ranks, rank starts to matter. And the higher the rank, the higher the appetite.

Bertrand Russell, looking at human behavior, said the deep, driving hungers in fallen people are acquisitiveness, rivalry, vanity, and the love of power. You don't need a theological education to see how those four ride into the church the minute you build a hierarchy.

- Acquisitiveness — control of money, property, prestige.
- Rivalry — jockeying for appointment, title, influence, favor.
- Vanity — robes, seats of honor, being called "Father," "Your Eminence," "Your Excellency," "Prince of the Church."
- Power — the ability to silence critics, protect insiders, and shape what truth gets told.

Once hierarchy hardened into habit, the distance between shepherd and sheep grew—and whenever distance grows, danger enters. The leadership begins to see itself as an elite class. The people are no longer a flock to be served; they become a base to be managed. That is how clericalism is born.

And once clericalism takes root, abuse is not a surprise. It is an inevitability. Where position is shielded from scrutiny, predators find cover. Where the reputation of the institution outranks the protection of the weak, judgment is already at the door.

Because when a system cares more about protecting the office than protecting the sheep, sin can hide in the robes. Men who should be defrocked, exposed, and handed over to authorities instead get moved, shielded, promoted. The machine starts serving itself.

Jesus saw that model coming from a mile off. He warned His disciples: *"You know that those regarded as rulers of the Gentiles lord it over them… but it shall not be so among you. Whoever wants to become great among you must be your servant, and whoever wants to be first must be the slave of all. For even the Son of Man did not come to be served, but to serve…"* (Mark 10:42–45).

Let's put that in plain dress:
- The world uses position. My church uses presence.
- The world climbs. My leaders kneel.

Montana Plain: "When the shepherd starts acting like a prince, the sheep are in danger."

4. The Modern Echo: From Pastor to Platform

Now, let's be honest. We Protestants like to point at Rome and say, "Look at that hierarchy." But we've built our own version. It just doesn't wear a miter. It wears skinny jeans and a mic.

The modern celebrity pastor is the evangelical echo of the medieval archbishop. Different wardrobe, same gravity well. Here's how it happens:
- The church grows.

- The pastor becomes "the brand."
- Systems form to protect access to the brand.
- The message becomes centralized in one personality.
- The elders stop acting like plural shepherds and start acting like a board of directors.
- Feedback stops flowing up. Accountability gets thin.
- Everyone else becomes support staff for "the vision."

That's hierarchy. We just swapped Latin for stage lighting.

You can see the shift in the vocabulary:
- From "pastor" to "lead pastor," then "senior pastor," then "founding pastor."
- From "congregation" to "audience."
- From "service" to "experience."
- From "saints doing the work of ministry" to "volunteers helping make Sunday happen."

Here is the quiet blasphemy in that: we reduce the work of the church to pulling off an event.

That is not Ephesians 4. That is event production. Ephesians 4 builds an army of servants; event culture builds a fan base. And in that model, the people of God are not equipped to minister in their daily world. They're equipped to park cars and hand out bulletins so the show runs on time.

Let me say this plainly: serving in the gathering matters. Order matters. Hospitality matters. Excellence matters. That's not the problem.

The problem is when we begin to believe that excellence in the gathering — the "experience" — is the mission. It is not.

The gathering is not the mission. The gathering is the refueling point for the mission.

Montana Plain: "Sunday morning is the campfire. Monday morning is the battlefield."

When the church forgets that, it turns inward. When it turns inward, it turns soft. And when it turns soft, it turns silent.

5. The Priesthood of All Believers — Not a Slogan, a Mandate

Now we come to the crux of the matter.

The New Testament teaches that every true believer is indwelt by the Holy Spirit. Not visited. Indwelt. The Spirit makes His home within the believer. Christ lives in us and through us. That means this: the presence of Christ is not bottled up in clergy. The presence of Christ is carried by the Body.

Peter didn't say, "Your clergy are a royal priesthood." He said to the whole church: "***You are a chosen people, a royal priesthood***" (1 Peter 2:9).

Paul didn't say, "The pastor will do the ministry while you watch." He said Christ gave pastor-teachers so that the saints would be equipped *"for the work of ministry"* (Ephesians 4:12).

Jesus didn't say, "A few of you will be my witnesses." He said, *"You shall be my witnesses... to the ends of the earth"* (Acts 1:8).

And in the Great Commission, the command is not "Go hold services." The command is *"make disciples."* The how is built into the wording: *"As you are going... baptizing... teaching them to observe all that I have commanded you..."* (Matt. 28:19–20).

"***As you are going.***" That's daily life. That's the shop, the classroom, the kitchen table, the patrol car, the hospital hallway, the tractor, the boardroom, the locker room, the drill site. Every believer is both witness and discipler. We do not just introduce people to Christ — we walk with them so they grow up in Christ.

Spectator Christianity is not a weaker version of the faith; it is a denial of our calling.

In other words, the church is not a weekly audience gathered to be impressed. The church is a deployed priesthood sent to bear witness.

Montana Plain: "The church isn't measured by its seating capacity. It's measured by its sending capacity."

6. Returning to the Real Church

So what does it look like to reclaim the real church?

It looks like this:

- Leaders go back to equipping, not performing. The pastor-teacher's main work is to train, steady, correct, strengthen, and prepare believers for real-world ministry — not just preach a polished talk and disappear into a green room.
- Elders go back to shepherding, not managing optics. They know the flock by name. They guard doctrine and character. They lead from the front with humility, not from behind a legal firewall.
- Deacons go back to serving through the dust. They meet needs in practical, humble, sacrificial ways so God's word and prayer are not neglected and no one in the flock is abandoned.
- The gathered church goes back to worship, fellowship, encouragement, communion, repentance, intercession, equipping.
- The scattered church goes back to witness, mercy, justice, reconciliation, truth-telling, gospel-bearing, disciple-making.

That is the rhythm: gather and strengthen; scatter and serve. If we get that rhythm back, the remnant rises. Because the remnant isn't defined by tax status, or denominational label, or seating chart, or streaming reach. The remnant is defined by obedience.

Montana Plain: "You don't have to fix everything to obey Jesus. You just have to obey Jesus."

7. The Call to Stand

Let's tell the truth: the big systems probably aren't going to fix themselves. Bureaucracies rarely repent. The machinery protects itself. The titles protect themselves. The money protects itself.

Reform might be hoped for. Restoration is what's available. Restoration happens when a single local congregation — just one lampstand — says:

- We will not imitate the world's ladder of power.
- We will treat leadership as service, not status.
- We will equip our people to live and speak Christ in daily life.
- We will measure faithfulness not by attendance but by obedience.
- We will expect every believer to be both a witness and a discipler.
- We will gather to worship, and we will scatter to work.
- We will not outsource the Great Commission.

That can happen in a church of 35 in a rental space. That can happen in a house church around a kitchen table. That can happen in a larger church that repents of performance and returns to mission. That can happen anywhere Christ is truly Lord and the Spirit truly indwells. Because Christ does not measure churches by size—only by obedience.

This is the priesthood of all believers:

- Christ as Head.
- The Spirit as indwelling power.
- Every believer as witness.

- Every calling as holy
- Every congregation as a lampstand under the direct gaze of Jesus Christ.

This is not nostalgia. This is not theory. This is New Testament Christianity.

And this is how we stand. Because a church built on hierarchy can be captured. But a church built on the indwelling Christ cannot.

This is the prophetic balance of *truth and tenderness* that the modern pulpit has lost. When Jesus opened Isaiah 61 in the synagogue — *"The Spirit of the Lord is upon me…"* — He embodied both halves of that calling: binding up the brokenhearted **and** proclaiming liberty to the captives. Comfort and confrontation. Grace and grit. Mercy and justice.

And what He did, we are to do.

For the priesthood of all believers to rise, the pulpit must return to the whole counsel of God.

Interlude: The Whole Counsel of God

"For I have not hesitated to proclaim to you the whole counsel of God." — Acts 20:27

Paul's farewell to the Ephesian elders was not nostalgia — it was testimony. He had discharged his duty. He had told them everything: the grace that saves, the judgment that purifies, the endurance that would be required. He had **not** trimmed the message to fit the mood of the crowd.

That is where we are failing today. Across America, pulpits have become **safe spaces**. The Gospel has been domesticated — soft edges, light tones, short attention spans. The prophetic fire that once shaped nations now flickers behind stage lights.

A generation ago, preachers were said to **comfort the afflicted and afflict the comfortable.**

Now, too many do neither. They soothe the comfortable and ignore the afflicted.

We have mistaken silence for civility. We have confused tact with truth. But as Paul told Timothy, *"Preach the Word; be ready in season and out of season; reprove, rebuke, exhort — with complete patience and teaching"* (2 Timothy 4:2).

The whole counsel of God includes the parts we prefer to skip — judgment, repentance, holiness, obedience. Grace means nothing unless we know what we've been saved from. If we will not stand where God stands — both for what He affirms and against what He condemns — then we are not His messengers, but our own.

Montana Plain: "Remember what we said, you can't be salt if you're worried about being sugar."

When pulpits go silent, the culture raises its voice—then turns up the volume. When shepherds whisper, wolves preach. The call on every pastor — and every believer — is to recover that holy tension: **comfort the afflicted, and afflict the comfortable.** To speak life to the wounded and truth to the wandering. To stand with Christ even when the crowd walks away.

For one day, every preacher will stand before the Audience of One. And He will not ask, "Did they like it?" He will ask, "Did you tell them?"

Montana Plain: "Better to be faithful and alone than famous and ashamed."

Stand to Purpose: The Priesthood in Motion

- Treat **every believer** as called, gifted, and sent. No spectators in this Kingdom.
- Shape gatherings as **equipping grounds**, not weekly shows.
- Tear down the **clergy–laity wall**: leaders equip; saints minister.
- Refuse platform culture: choose **plural shepherds over solitary stars**.
- Measure health by **obedience and sending**, not by attendance and applause.
- Preach the **whole counsel of God**—even the parts that thin the crowd.
- Remember: **Christ walks among lampstands, not brands.**

7

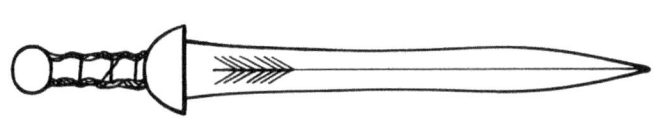

Life in the Spirit

This has always been the rule of battle: *'Not by might nor by power, but by My Spirit,' says the Lord of hosts"* (Zechariah 4:6).

The filling of the Spirit is continual yieldedness, not an event.

This is endurance over theatrics; Presence over adrenaline.

1. We Will Not Stand in the Flesh

We've spent the first half of this book naming the collapse — truth assassinated, institutions captured, pulpits silenced, the church seduced by performance and power. Now we come to the point that decides our future: ***you cannot stand in this present darkness in your own strength***.

You might have doctrine. You might have willpower. You might have conservative instincts. You might be angry at what's happening in the schools, the halls of power, even the churches. That's not enough.

The early church did not endure Rome, mobs, prison, exile, slander, and death because they "tried harder." They endured because they were indwelt and continually filled by the Holy Spirit — and they lived yielded to Him.

We've talked about the remnant, the faithful lampstands. Here's the truth that sits under that: the remnant is not just doctrinally faithful, it is spiritually surrendered.

Montana Plain: "Grit alone won't carry you through the fire. You're gonna need God in you, not just ideas about Him."

This chapter is about that — Life in the Spirit. Not an event. Not a flash of emotion. Not a conference high. A life.

2. Yieldedness: The Posture of a Disciple

Paul gave the church a word that many modern believers have never really wrestled with: ***yield***.

Romans 6:13 —*"Do not go on presenting the parts of your body to sin as instruments of unrighteousness, but present yourselves to God as those alive from the dead, and your members as instruments of righteousness to God."* (NASB1977)

That word "present" — *yield* — carries the idea of ongoing offering. Not a moment, a posture. Paul is saying:

- Stop handing yourself to sin.
- Start handing yourself — your mind, tongue, habits, energy, relationships, appetites, money, time — to God.
- Do it as people who have already crossed from death to life.

That same theme explodes again in Romans 12:1–2: *"I urge you therefore, brothers, by the mercies of God, to present your bodies a living and holy sacrifice... this is your spiritual service of worship. And do not be conformed to this world, but be transformed by the renewing of your mind..."*

Slow this down.

- "***By the mercies of God.***" We don't yield out of guilt. We yield out of gratitude. We're not trying to earn God's favor. We've already received mercy.
- "***Present your bodies.***" God isn't just after your "spiritual life." He wants your actual life — speech, desires, appetites, schedule, browser, wallet, reactions, tone of voice, how you handle pressure. No split between sacred and secular. All of you on the altar, all week long.
- "***Do not be conformed.***" Paul literally says: Don't let the world press you into its mold. Don't take on its shape, its reflexes, its values.
- "***Be transformed.***" *Metamorphousthe* — same root we use for metamorphosis. The caterpillar to the butterfly. Not a tune-up. A rebirth in motion.

Yieldedness is not passivity. It's not lying on the floor waiting to feel something; it's getting up and placing every part of life at God's disposal. Yieldedness is active surrender. It is decisive. It is practical. It is daily. "Here I am, Lord. Take my thoughts. Take my words. Take my hands. Take my time. Take my fears. Take my anger. Take my plans. They're Yours, not mine."

Montana Plain: "If you want the Spirit to steer, you gotta take your hands off the wheel."

This is the ground floor of Life in the Spirit.

3. Life in the Spirit Is Not Religious Performance
Right here we have to draw a thick line between religion and life in Christ.
- Religion says: keep the rules, manage the optics, mind your

behavior, maintain membership in good standing, stay inside the lines, check the boxes.
- Christianity says: you were dead, and God made you alive.
- Religion tries to climb up to God.
- The Gospel says God came down to us.
- Religion says, "Do."
- Christ says, "Done."
- Religion is about managing appearances.
- Christianity is about restored relationship.

And that relationship is alive because of the Spirit.

Jesus promised His followers that the Spirit would come, not to drop in on weekends, but to indwell — *"to be with you forever… for He dwells with you and will be in you"* (John 14:16–17). That's permanent language. That's covenant language. He told them the Spirit would teach them, remind them, lead them into truth, even show them what is to come (John 14:26; 16:13). That is not ritual. That is companionship.

Montana Plain: "The Spirit doesn't check in. He moves in."

This is why we say: standing in this age is not about "being religious." It's about living under the moment-by-moment influence of the Spirit of God who lives in you.

4. Baptism in the Spirit: Life Begun

Let's untangle two words that get confused, abused, and marketed: baptism and filling.

First, **baptism** of the Holy Spirit. Paul writes: *"For by one Spirit we were all baptized into one body… and we were all made to drink of one Spirit."* (1 Corinthians 12:13)

Four core truths fall right out of that verse:

1. The Spirit's baptism is common to all believers. Paul says *"we were all baptized."* Not the "special few." Not the spiritually elite. All. The church is not divided into "those who have the Spirit" and "those who don't." If you are in Christ, the Spirit has placed you into His Body.

2. The Spirit's baptism is already accomplished. *"Were… baptized."* Past tense. Aorist. Completed action. Spirit baptism is not a prize you chase later. It is something God did in you when He saved you — when He took you from death to life.

3. The Spirit's baptism makes you part of Christ. We are *"baptized into one body."* You don't join the Body of Christ by paperwork. You are joined by the Spirit's act. He seals you as God's own. He indwells you. He marks you as belonging to Christ. You are *"in Christ"* and Christ is in you.

4. The Spirit's baptism erases status walls. *"Jews or Greeks, slaves or free."* In other words, ethnicity, class, social rank — none of that outranks union with Christ. The Spirit levels the ground.

So, let's be clear: Spirit baptism is God's act of making you alive in Christ and joining you to His Body. It happens at salvation. It is once-for-all. It is not repeated. It is not a merit badge. It is not a conference experience. It is the birth of spiritual life.

This matters because we are surrounded by noise in the modern church world telling people to "seek the baptism" like it's an upgrade package. That teaching often confuses (or blends) what Scripture distinguishes.

At salvation, the Spirit indwells you. Permanently. Seals you. Marks you. Makes you His.

That is settled.

Now we talk about the second word--*filling*.

If baptism is once-for-all union, filling is ongoing surrender.

5. Filling with the Spirit: Life Surrendered

Baptism is about the Spirit taking hold of you.
Filling is about you letting the Spirit take over.

In Ephesians 5:18, Paul writes: "*Do not get drunk with wine... but be filled with the Spirit.*" We've heard that verse so often we miss the force of it. Paul is saying: Just like alcohol can dominate a person's speech, emotions, walk, reflexes, judgment — so the Holy Spirit should dominate you. He should be the prevailing influence. The controlling presence. The operating system.

> Some have said, "*Being filled affects how you walk, how you talk, how you feel, and how you spend—just like a drunk. If you're going to be drunk, be drunk on the Spirit, not on spirits!*"

That single phrase "be filled" (*plerousthe*) carries four truths we dare not water down:

1. **It's a command**. This is not a suggestion for the especially devout. It's an imperative. "Be filled." To refuse a command of God and call it humility is not humility. It's disobedience.
2. **It's plural**. Paul isn't talking to pastors only. He's talking to the entire congregation. All of you — be filled. There are no second-class saints. The filling of the Spirit is normal Christianity, not advanced Christianity.
3. **It's passive**. "Be filled" means you do not fill yourself. You yield to be filled. You allow Him to take control. He won't bulldoze a locked heart. The issue is surrender.
4. **It's continuous**. The tense is present, ongoing: "Keep on being filled." This is not a one-time zap. This is a daily, hourly, moment-by-moment yielding to His control.

Put together, we get this: "I command all of you: allow yourselves, constantly, to be being filled with the Spirit." That's Life in the Spirit.

Montana Plain: "The Spirit isn't a firework. He's a furnace."

This destroys two modern errors at once:
- The emotionalist error: treating the Spirit like an occasional adrenaline hit.
- The institutional error: treating the Spirit like a doctrine you sign off on but never actually submit to.

The biblical picture is neither hype nor dryness. It is ongoing, surrendered control. Too often our songs and prayers speak as though the Spirit were still outside us—asking Him to "rain down" or be "poured out." But the truth is, the Spirit already dwells within every believer. What we need is not another descent, but deeper surrender.

The filling of the Spirit is not about Him falling, as at Pentecost—that was a once-for-all event, like the Resurrection. It is about an upwelling from within as we yield. The Lordship of Christ is expressed through our daily yieldedness to the Spirit who abides in us.

Montana Plain: "The Fire of Pentecost fell once. Now that fire rises from within each follower of Jesus."

6. Relationship vs. Fellowship

Here's a distinction that will save some confusion: relationship and fellowship.
- Relationship with God never changes for believers. When we are redeemed, sealed, indwelt — that is settled. We belong to Christ. The Spirit is in us forever (John 14:16–17). We are His.

- Fellowship with God absolutely changes. Fellowship can be rich in the morning and broken by noon. We can walk in yieldedness today and sulk in the flesh tomorrow. We can pray in faith in one moment and snap in anger the next.

That's why ongoing filling matters. Filling isn't "Do I still have the Spirit?" Filling is "Am I letting Him have me?" That's why Paul ties filling to practical, observable outcomes in Ephesians 5:19–21:

- Worship instead of grumbling.
- Gratitude instead of entitlement.
- Mutual submission instead of ego.

It's not spooky. It's not theatrical. It's visible character.

7. The Fruit of the Spirit: The Character of Christ in a Human Life

Now — what does a Spirit-filled life actually look like?

Paul answers in Galatians 5:22–23 with what he calls "the fruit of the Spirit": love, joy, peace, patience, kindness, goodness, faithfulness, gentleness, self-control.

A few things we absolutely must say:

First, fruit is singular.

Paul does not say "fruits," plural. He says "fruit." That means this isn't a buffet. You don't say, "I'll take joy and peace, but I'm not really into patience." The fruit is one thing — the character of Jesus produced in us — with nine facets.

Second, fruit is grown, not manufactured.

Paul contrasts "the works of the flesh" with "the fruit of the Spirit." Works are what the flesh produces in its own effort. Fruit is what grows naturally out of union with Christ. The branch doesn't manufacture grapes. It abides in the vine and the life of the vine produces fruit.

Jesus said it in John 15: "I am the vine; you are the branches... apart from Me you can do nothing." Branches don't generate fruit. They bear it. They carry it.

Third, the fruit of the Spirit is not emotion. It's resemblance.

It is the likeness of Christ formed in the believer through yieldedness, over time. Let's walk the nine quickly through a framework of triads—

First comes how we stand before God:
- **Love (agape):** Seeking the other's good even when they don't seek yours. God-like, cross-shaped love. This is not "niceness." It's covenant loyalty. It is self-sacrificing love.
- **Joy:** Not giddiness. Joy is stability of heart rooted in relationship with Christ, not in circumstance. Paul could rejoice in prison because of the abiding presence of Christ in him.
- **Peace:** Settled well-being that comes from being right with God and aligned with His will. Not "no conflict," but "rightly ordered soul." This is what Paul stated as the result of the right standing before God that the believer has because of the death of Christ on behalf of sinners (Romans 3:10-26). Through faith in Christ, God pronounces us to have a right standing before Him. And when we exchange our sin for His righteousness, we have restoration of peace (Romans 5:1-11).

These three — love, joy, peace — are like foundation stones. They free us to care for others without being ruled by fear.

Then comes how we treat others:

- **Patience:** Slowness to retaliate when wronged. Choosing not to match the volume of the world.
- **Kindness:** Softness of spirit, a nonabrasive presence. Kindness is mercy expressed. It has about it a mellow character. This is the same word that Jesus used of His yoke—*Take My yoke upon you, and learn from Me, for I am gentle and humble in heart; and you shall find rest for your souls. For My yoke is easy, and My load is light* (Mt. 11:29-30). When Jesus spoke of His yoke being easy, He used the word for kindness. His yoke fits without chafing, irking, or galling. So is kindness.
- **Goodness:** Righteous action in motion. Not just a warm tone; sometimes a firm hand on the rudder. Jesus with the woman caught in adultery — kindness. Jesus flipping tables in the Temple — goodness. Same Lord.

Then comes how we walk before God:
- **Faithfulness:** Steadfast loyalty. Dependability in the long run. Staying at your post. *"I have kept the faith."*
- **Gentleness / Meekness:** Power under control. Like a team of oxen able to crush their handler but choosing disciplined obedience instead. That's Christlike strength, not weakness.
- **Self-control:** Holding yourself in hand. The boxer who doesn't waste punches. The runner who stays in his lane. The saint who refuses the impulse of the flesh because he's living under a higher rule.

That last cluster matters in our time. The age we live in celebrates the unrestrained self. The Spirit produces the governed self.

At the end of his life, Paul doesn't brag about his resume. He says this: *"I have fought the good fight. I have finished the race. I have kept the faith"* (2 Timothy 4:7).

That is Spirit-formed endurance. That's what we're after. That's what the remnant looks like when it's old and scarred and faithful.

Not flashy. Faithful.
Not loud. Steady.
Not famous. Obedient.

Montana Plain: "In the end, the crown doesn't go to the popular. It goes to the proven. Hell does not fear our platforms; it fears our fruit."

8. Pentecost Was Not a Show

Let's go back to Pentecost for a minute. Acts 2 is often preached today like it was mainly about spectacle — wind, fire, languages. But Pentecost was far more than the sum of the phenomenon that occurred.

On Pentecost, two things happened at once:

1. The Spirit ***baptized*** believers into one Body. The church was birthed in sound and fury as the Spirit came in power.
2. Those believers were ***filled*** — totally yielded, totally available, totally under His control.

That moment was unique in salvation history. There will only ever be one Pentecost, just as there will only ever be one Resurrection Sunday.

But while that *moment* is not repeatable, the *posture* is absolutely repeatable. Those early believers were so yielded, so open — that the Spirit had full access to them. And what flowed out of that wasn't just images of wind and fire. It was life together.

Recall the portrait of the early church from Acts 2:42–47:

- Continued in the apostles' teaching.
- Continued in fellowship.

- Continued in breaking of bread and prayer.
- Met needs among themselves sacrificially.
- Worshiped with gladness and sincerity.
- Saw favor and growth as the Lord added daily those who were being saved.

That's the portrait of a Spirit-filled church: Teaching. Fellowship. Worship. Care. Witness.

Notice what's missing: fog machines, brand, marketing taglines, personal platforms, curated personality cults. If what we call "anointed" leaves God's people unchanged and immobilized, it is not a movement of the Spirit's power—it is production.

The fruit of filling is not hype. It's holiness. It's mutual care. It's bold witness. It's daily faithfulness. That's our model for life in the Spirit.

9. Where This Brings Us

We said this at the start of the chapter, and now we can say it with more weight: Standing in this hour is not about anger at the culture. It's about surrender to the Spirit.

If we are going to speak with courage, resist compromise, live clean in a filthy age, raise truth against lies, and endure hardship without folding — we cannot do that in the flesh. The flesh can rage. The flesh can rant. The flesh can posture. But the flesh cannot endure.

Only the Spirit can produce endurance without bitterness, boldness without arrogance, conviction without hatred, joy without denial, and holiness without self-righteousness.

That's Life in the Spirit:
- Baptized into Christ once-for-all at salvation.
- Filled continually as we yield.

- Bearing fruit as His character is formed in us.
- Walking in daily fellowship, not weekend religion.
- Standing in power that is not our own.

This is where the remnant gets its strength. This is where the church gets her witness back. This is how we stop being spectators and start being saints.

Montana Plain: "It's not about getting more of the Spirit. It's about the Spirit getting more of you."

The war in which we are engaged is at its core a spiritual war: *For we do not wrestle against flesh and blood, but against the rulers, against the authorities, against the cosmic powers over this present darkness, against the spiritual forces of evil in the heavenly places* (Eph. 6:12). The only way for a warrior to engage that warfare is to do so prepared by our baptism in the Spirit which makes us a child of the King and a member of the Body of Christ and prepared by our yieldedness to the Spirit by which we are filled and fruitful. Only then are we prepared to put on the armor of God and engage the enemy.

Going into battle without surrendering to the Spirit, without His filling, is like taking a rifle with no cartridges into the fight.

Everything we've said about Life in the Spirit is not mystical abstraction; it is preparation for war.

Stand to Purpose: Live Fully Yielded

- Trust your **once-for-all baptism in the Spirit**; stop chasing upgrades and start walking in what's done.
- Obey the command: ***"Be filled with the Spirit"***—daily, consciously, repentantly.

- Refuse theatrical substitutes: measure "anointing" by **holiness, endurance, and fruit**—not by volume or vibe.
- Guard **fellowship**: keep short accounts with God; when you grieve the Spirit, repent quickly and return.
- Pursue the **fruit of the Spirit** as if it were battle armor—love, joy, peace, and the rest as the character that stands when the storm hits.
- Remember the war: *"Not by might, nor by power, but by My Spirit."* Stand where He stands, in the strength He supplies.

8

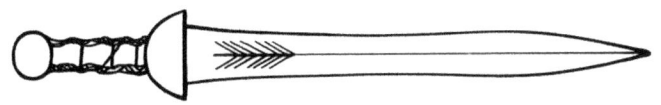

Seven Disciplines of Personal Discipleship

"Discipline is the soul of an army. It makes small numbers formidable, procures success for the weak, and esteem for all."
General George Washington

If anyone would come after me, let him deny himself and take up his cross daily and follow me.
--Jesus, Luke 9:23

Before a soldier ever straps on the armor, before he ever sets foot on the battlefield, he endures the training necessary for the army. Most services have some form of boot camp. In boot camp the recruit is shaped mentally and physically. The recruit is given the skills necessary to engage the enemy.

Boot camp breaks a man before it builds him. It tears down comfort, excuses, and pride until discipline replaces impulse. So it is with the follower of Christ. The Spirit drills us through daily obedience, shaping our reflexes for righteousness. We are not trained for parade ground religion but for battlefield endurance.

For the Christian, our boot camp is the disciplines of the Christian faith. Some of these are collective disciplines—public worship and fellowship. But many of these are the disciplines of the faith that are practiced in private by each individual follower of Christ. And these are ***daily*** disciplines, just as the recruit had daily physical training and training in handling of weapons, the Christian warrior has daily, individual disciplines they need to practice.

Jesus said, "*If anyone would come after me, let him deny himself and take up his cross **daily** and follow me* (Luke 9:23)." Often this is misquoted because the word ***"daily"*** is omitted. That word is crucial. It needs to be stressed. For it is in the daily disciplines that the soldier's actions and responses are ingrained, becoming response without thought. They become reflex.

This is no different than any sport or activity where time is not given for thought. The response must be immediate and reflexive. So an action is repeated again and again until the response is ingrained in muscle memory. Instead of thinking, reflex takes over. And that can be the difference between victory and defeat. In the time one opponent has to stop and think what the next move should be, the other has cut him down. But if an action is repeated and repeated—again and again, no thought is required. Immediate response gives victory.

Ask the greats, where the flawless performance is born and they will tell you that the victory was won in practice. It matters not the sport or the activity. For the singer it is singing scales. For the golfer, it is in swinging the club and hitting thousands of balls. For Larry Bird, it was shooting shots from every spot on the court thousands of times. For Jimi Hendrix, it was living with the guitar and playing it until it became an extension of his soul.

Victory is in the daily practice of disciplines. And so it is with the Christian warrior. Our proficiency in battle comes from the daily disciplines of the faith.

"Every army trains before it fights, and every follower of Christ must learn the disciplines that turn conviction into courage. No army wins with untrained soldiers, and no church stands with undisciplined saints."

The Practice of Spiritual Disciplines

Discipleship has always been personal before it is ever public. The life of faith does not begin in the crowd or the committee; it begins in the quiet space between the believer and God. These seven disciplines — from prayer to Bible study — are the foundations of that private walk. They are not dependent upon church programs, clergy leadership, or the presence of others. Each is sustained in solitude, refined in obedience, and empowered by the Spirit who dwells within every believer.

The church can enhance these practices, but it cannot replace them. Collective worship, shared encouragement, and community fellowship all serve to strengthen the believer's resolve — but none of them can substitute for personal devotion. In the end, discipleship is about a man or woman who practices daily the spiritual disciplines of following Jesus. The Body of Christ is built from individuals who first learned to stand before God alone. The strength of the church depends upon the strength of its members in those unseen places where faith is proven one decision at a time.

Followship is a word worth reclaiming. It reminds us that discipleship is not just believing the right things, but following the right Person. To follow Christ is to pursue Him daily — in prayer, in thought, in attitude, in action. Fellowship flows from followship. The gathering of the faithful becomes meaningful only when each heart within it has already learned to walk with God in the secret place.

These seven disciplines form the backbone of that journey.

Prayer begins the conversation; meditation deepens understanding; yieldedness brings surrender; stewardship expresses responsibility; witness shares the hope within; gifts-based ministry gives that hope form and function; and Bible study anchors it all in truth. Practiced together, they cultivate spiritual maturity that stands firm when everything else trembles.

The pages that follow are not prescriptions for religion but invitations to relationship — not a system of control but a way of life shaped by grace and personal commitment. This is what it means to be a disciple of Jesus Christ: to walk with Him daily, personally, faithfully — even when no one else is watching.

1. The Discipline of Prayer
Core Truth:
Prayer is the believer's lifeline to God — not a ritual but a relationship. It's the ongoing conversation between Creator and creature, where gratitude, confession, and petition draw the soul into alignment with divine purpose.

Practice:
True prayer begins with honesty. It isn't performance but presence — speaking with God as with a trusted friend. Regular time set apart, free from distraction, trains the heart to listen as much as to speak. Scripture-anchored prayers, quiet reflection, and intercession for others turn prayer from duty to delight. Over time, a pattern emerges: the believer prays not merely for outcomes, but for the will of God to take root within.

Illustration:
When Elisha's servant trembled before the Syrian army at Dothan, the prophet prayed, "Lord, open his eyes." Suddenly the young man saw the hills ablaze with horses and chariots of fire.

Prayer didn't change the situation first — it changed perception. Likewise, George Washington Carver began each day walking into the Alabama woods, praying, "Lord, show me the mysteries of the peanut."

And show him God did—Dr. Carver became one of the most notable chemists of his day. Working in the laboratory at Tuskegee Institute, which he affectionately called "God's Little Workshop," he developed over 300 innovative uses for the peanut as well as breakthroughs in the use of sweet potatoes, pecans and soybeans. His efforts in chemistry and food science paved the way for the growth of a peanut industry. In his day peanuts were often used for little more than animal feed, but today it has grown into a two-billion-dollar market domestically.

His discoveries were born of that morning communion, not calculation.

Fruit:
Prayer reshapes a person from the inside out. Worry gives way to trust. Fear yields to peace. From the prophet who saw the invisible to the scientist who listened to the whisper of creation, prayer remains the place where human limitation meets divine abundance. The believer who prays consistently learns that the act itself is the answer — communion with God that steadies the spirit when foundations shake.

Reflection for the Road:
Prayer opens the gate to the unseen; through it, the believer learns that talking with God is the truest form of seeing.

From the stillness of prayer, the heart turns naturally to meditation — the place where listening becomes living, and hearing gives birth to doing.

2. The Discipline of Meditation
Core Truth:
Meditation is the bridge between knowing God's word and living it. It isn't emptying the mind but *filling it* with truth until it seeps into thought, speech, and behavior.

Practice:
Biblical meditation means turning a verse or passage over in the mind — chewing it like bread for the soul — until its meaning becomes personal and transforming. Quiet moments of reflection, walks in solitude, or journaling through Scripture all help truth move from head to heart. The discipline lies not in length but in focus; a single verse, rightly pondered, can recalibrate an entire day or even an entire life.

Illustration:
Meditation is a continual discipline — a day-and-night rhythm of ***musing*** and ***muttering***. The psalmist spoke of it in Psalm 1 and God told Joshua not to let the word of God depart from his mouth (Joshua 1: 8). The Hebrew idea captures both thought and speech — what the heart ponders, the lips quietly repeat. Out here in Montana, it's like a cow working its cud: drawing nourishment from what's already been taken in. Truth is turned and turned again until every ounce of strength is drawn from it.

Fruit:
Meditation cultivates a renewed mind and a centered life. It slows the hurried pace of the world, making room for wisdom and discernment. Meditation is not a single act but a sustained appetite. It is musing and muttering — pondering and repeating truth until it becomes reflex.

In this discipline, Scripture moves from print to pulse. Those who meditate on God's word discover stability; they are, as the psalmist said, *"like a tree planted by streams of water,"* nourished and unshaken, rooted and fruitful.

Reflection for the Road:
Meditation turns the word of God over until it becomes part of you — what begins in the mind ends in the marrow.

What the believer learns in meditation prepares the heart for surrender. The next step in followship is not understanding, but obedience — the discipline of yieldedness.

3. The Discipline of Yieldedness
Core Truth:
Yieldedness is the daily decision to surrender self-will to God's will. It's where faith becomes obedience and belief becomes trust.

Practice:
Yieldedness begins when the believer acknowledges that the throne belongs to God alone. It's practiced in moments both grand and small — choosing grace over retaliation, obedience over convenience, humility over pride. Each act of surrender is a quiet declaration: "Not my will, but Yours be done." Yieldedness isn't weakness; it's strength under control, guided by the Spirit.

Illustration:
Mary's simple assent — *"Be it unto me according to Thy word"* — and Christ's prayer in Gethsemane reveal that surrender is not resignation but trust. This trust is found in the Philippi jail where Paul and Silas were praying and singing in the midnight hour. In a later age, Corrie ten Boom displayed that same yieldedness behind barbed wire, whispering hymns in the darkness.

Yieldedness is not passive; it's the poise of obedience.

Whether in Gethsemane or in a prison cell, the yielded heart whispers, "Thy will be done," and heaven hears.

Fruit:
A yielded life radiates peace and purpose. The Spirit fills what the self vacates. Over time, the believer becomes more Christlike — not because of effort alone, but because the surrendered heart becomes the vessel through which God's power flows freely.

Reflection for the Road:
Yieldedness is not giving up, but giving over — the release of control that lets God take the reins.

What we yield to God in surrender becomes the foundation of stewardship. The hands that have released control are now ready to manage what they've been given.

"Once you've laid it all on the altar, you're ready to hold it with open hands."

4. The Discipline of Stewardship
Core Truth:
Stewardship is the recognition that everything we possess — time, talent, treasure, and even influence — belongs to God. We are not owners but caretakers, accountable for how we invest what has been entrusted to us.

Practice:
True stewardship begins with gratitude and grows through responsibility. It means managing resources with wisdom, giving generously, and serving faithfully. The question shifts from "How much must I give?" to "How much can I use for God's glory?" Whether through finances, abilities, or opportunities, the steward asks how each choice reflects the Master's priorities.

Illustration:
The parable of the talents shows that faithful stewardship multiplies what is placed in our hands. Joseph's care of Pharaoh's storehouses preserved nations. In more recent times, men and women who have seen themselves as stewards rather than owners — business leaders funding missions, farmers tithing their harvest, families opening their homes — have proven that generosity multiplies. Every gift and opportunity carries the echo of the Master's trust.

Fruit:
Stewardship produces freedom and joy. The grip of materialism loosens and contentment takes root. The faithful steward learns that generosity multiplies rather than diminishes — that in God's economy, what is given in love returns as grace and blessing, pressed down and running over. It is the small lunch of a young lad that in the hands of the Lord feeds the multitude.

Reflection for the Road:
Stewardship is gratitude in action — the daily management of grace entrusted to our hands. "It is required of stewards that they be found faithful." (Apostle Paul to the Corinthians—1 Cor. 4:2)

From stewardship flows witness. For what we manage well in private becomes our testimony in public. The next discipline gives faith a voice — the discipline of witness.

5. The Discipline of Witness
Core Truth:
Witness is the outward expression of an inward transformation. It is both testimony and lifestyle — the way believers make Christ visible in word and deed.

Practice:
Witness begins with integrity. Before we speak, we live. The believer's kindness, patience, and courage prepare the soil for the Gospel. Yet words matter too; faith must be spoken. Sharing Christ is not about winning arguments but offering hope. Each conversation, act of service, and prayer for others becomes part of the divine dialogue through which God draws hearts to Himself.

Illustration:
Peter and John, standing before the Sanhedrin, said, *"We cannot but speak of what we have seen and heard."* That same courage animated Dietrich Bonhoeffer, who bore witness to truth in the face of Hitler's tyranny. Witness is word and wound — the courage to speak, and even to suffer, for the truth that sets men free.

In September 2025, I watched the memorial for Charlie Kirk in Phoenix. Hundreds of thousands gathered — two full arenas inside, thousands more outside in the desert heat. They came not merely to honor a leader, but to testify. Speaker after speaker rose to say what mattered most: that Charlie's hope was not in himself, but in Christ.

Scripture calls believers in Jesus Christ ***saints*** — not because of heroic deeds or posthumous recognition, but because God Himself has set them apart through their faith. Jude addresses believers not as achievers but as the acted-upon—called, loved, and kept by God. In the earliest texts, he emphasizes divine love and preservation; in others, sanctification itself. Whether Jude speaks of believers as "loved" or "sanctified," the idea is the same: they are *hagios*—set apart by God's action, not elevated by human recognition.

- We do not become saints by faithful stewardship.
- We steward because we already are saints.

Witness flows from identity, not aspiration. Sainthood is God's declaration before it is ever our demonstration.

It was not the event of Charlie Kirk's death that made him a saint, but the faith that oriented his life. His friends and admirers did not confer that status; God did — long before the shot was fired.

His death did not create his witness; it revealed it. His death did not make him a martyr; his life as a witness had already done that. The Greek word for *witness* is *martys*. To bear witness, even to the point of death, is to affirm something higher than survival.

That is what Kierkegaard meant when he wrote, "The tyrant dies and his rule is over; the martyr dies and his rule begins." The tyrant's power ends with his breath; the martyr's begins when his breath is taken.

Fruit:
A witnessing life brings renewal — both to others and to the witness. Joy deepens when faith is shared. Communities change when light replaces silence. The believer who bears witness becomes a living letter of grace, read by all who watch how faith behaves when tested.

Reflection for the Road:
Witness is the sound of faith breathing in public — the testimony of a life anchored in eternal hope. If your faith won't speak, your silence will condemn not only the lost but your reward as well.

May we be faithful to our Lord in word and deed so that every opportunity is taken to serve Him and seek the lost.

When Christ walks among the lampstands, He is not counting heads; He is counting witnesses.

Montana Plain: "A church that stays inside the barn too long forgets what it means to plow."

The believer who witnesses learns quickly that no one serves alone. The next discipline moves from message to ministry — how our gifts find purpose in service.

6. The Discipline of Gifts-Based Ministry
Core Truth:
Every believer is uniquely gifted by the Holy Spirit to serve within the Body of Christ. Ministry flows not from title or position but from spiritual giftedness — grace expressed through service.

Practice:
Discovering one's gifts begins with humility and willingness. The believer asks, "How has God shaped me to help others grow?" Through prayer, study, and feedback from the community, gifts are identified, developed, and deployed. The goal is not personal recognition but corporate edification — the church functioning as a living organism, each part doing its share in harmony. (Use the Spiritual Gifts Inventory in the Appendix—beginning on page 215—to help you know your giftedness.)

Illustration:
Paul described the Body of Christ as a living organism — eye, hand, and foot all necessary to the whole. In the same way a young wrangler learns from an older hand, believers learn to exercise their gifts through mentorship and service. The church is a workshop, not a warehouse. Gifts grow by being used. Each believer is both apprentice and craftsman in the artistry of grace.

God has given each of us as followers of Jesus certain, specific gifts that equip us for ministry. Paul expressed it this way in his first epistle to the Corinthian believers:

4Now there are varieties of gifts, but the same Spirit; 5and there are varieties of service, but the same Lord; **6***and there are varieties of activities, but it is the same God who empowers them all in everyone.* **7To each is given the manifestation of the Spirit for the common good.** **8***For to one is given through the Spirit the utterance of wisdom, and to another the utterance of knowledge according to the same Spirit,* **9***to another faith by the same Spirit, to another gifts of healing by the one Spirit,* **10***to another the working of miracles, to another prophecy, to another the ability to distinguish between spirits, to another various kinds of tongues, to another the interpretation of tongues.* **11All these are empowered by one and the same Spirit, who apportions to each one individually as he wills** (1 Cor. 12:4-11).

Within the combination of gifts God has given is the ministry He wants each of us to perform. The Apostle Peter recorded that each of us has a stewardship of our giftedness to the One who gave them: **10***As each has received a gift, use it to serve one another,* **as good stewards of God's varied grace**: **11***whoever speaks, as one who speaks oracles of God; whoever serves, as one who serves by the strength that God supplies—in order that in everything God may be glorified through Jesus Christ. To him belong glory and dominion forever and ever. Amen* (1 Peter 4:10-11).

"The Spirit's gifts are not trophies to admire but tools to use. A tool rusts without work; a gift withers without service."

Fruit:
When gifts are exercised in love, the Body thrives. Unity replaces competition, and joy replaces fatigue. The believer finds fulfillment not in being noticed but in being useful — the deep satisfaction of knowing that God's grace and power have found a channel through human hands.

Reflection for the Road:
Ministry is grace made visible — the art of turning giftedness into service for the good of all.

From ministry we return to the foundation — the word of God that informs, corrects, and renews all the rest. The final discipline brings us back to the bedrock: the study of Scripture.

7. The Discipline of Bible Study
Core Truth:
Bible study is the anchor of spiritual life — the means by which believers hear God's voice, understand His ways, and align their steps with His truth. Scripture is not merely a record of divine words; it is the living word of God, active and transformative.

Practice:
Effective study combines reverence with method. The believer reads prayerfully, observes context, asks questions, and applies lessons personally. Scripture study is not about collecting information but experiencing transformation. Regular, disciplined engagement with God's word forms spiritual muscle memory — shaping thought, conviction, and action.

Illustration:
Ezra "*set his heart to study the Law of the Lord, to do it, and to teach.*" George Washington Carver began each day with an open Bible beside his laboratory bench, convinced that God's world and God's word spoke the same truth in two languages. Study is more than reading; it is relationship through revelation. The Bible is not just a book to master — it is the Voice that masters us.

Dr. Kevin Peacock, Professor of Old Testament at the Canadian Southern Baptist Seminary, offers insight into this principle.

He outlines this principle like this:

"We call the Bible 'God's word,' and by that we mean that God has something to say. We believe that God wants people to understand His word and is not trying to be obscure. He spoke to people in the past and He wants to speak to people today through His word. Therefore, we can study the Bible with the knowledge and hope that God wants to speak to us. In fact, any person of normal intelligence under the illumination of the Holy Spirit can understand and apply God's word.

A common sense approach to biblical interpretation assumes that the primary meaning of any passage is the meaning that the biblical author intended. This "historical meaning" should control all other meanings anyone may find. The Scripture cannot mean what it did not mean. Therefore, we seek to answer three questions in each passage:

(1) What did it mean to the original author and audience? Reading the passage in its context, Bible reference notes, commentaries, and dictionaries will help you find this information.

(2) What does it mean? (i.e. What timeless truths are found here? Bible cross references, study notes, and commentaries will help you find some of this, but prayer and openness to God's Spirit is your main resource here.

(3) What does it mean today? Getting to know yourself and your audience will allow the Holy Spirit to draw a connection between people's needs and this passage.

A very important principle is necessary to note here: this last question should not be answered until the previous two have been answered. Once you have found the lasting truth in the passage, then you can apply the truth to today's setting.

Fruit:
The word of God builds endurance and discernment. It anchors

faith in storms and guards the mind from deception. Over time, it renews the heart until obedience becomes instinctive. Bible study is where the believer learns again and again that God's truth stands firm — unshaken, even when everything else trembles.

Reflection for the Road:
Study until the word studies you — let truth do its deep work until you find yourself reading it from the inside out.

(See page 238 in the Appendix for "A Bible Reading Guide for Those Who Are Called to Stand.")

The Rhythm of Discipline: From Method to Movement

The practice of disciplined devotion is not new. From the apostles to the early church fathers, from desert monastics to reformers like John and Charles Wesley, believers have long sought ordered ways to grow in grace. The Wesleys, in particular, believed that methodical devotion—hence the name *Methodists*—could train believers to holiness. They emphasized prayer, fasting, Scripture reading, witness, stewardship, and mutual accountability as habits that shaped the soul for godliness.

Yet there is a danger in mistaking rhythm for rigidity. What began as holy order can easily harden into human routine. The disciplines were never meant to be mechanical rows pulled against an indifferent current, but sails lifted to catch the breath—the *pneuma*—of the Spirit. Rowing depends on muscle; sailing depends on wind. Both require attention, but one strains to move forward while the other yields to power beyond itself.

This is the difference between religion and relationship, between method and movement, between rowing and sailing. The goal of discipline is not to prove devotion but to position the heart to be moved by divine Presence.

What the Wesleys sought through structure, the Spirit now invites us to experience as an *incarnational rhythm of discipleship*—grace infused into daily life until prayer becomes breath, meditation becomes thought, witness becomes reflex, and obedience becomes joy.

In the early stages, we row—learning form and effort. But once the wind of the Spirit fills the sails, the motion becomes natural, fluid, joyful. The disciplines still steer the vessel, but grace provides the wind.

Infused disciplines feel like the New Testament's own cadence—*kairos* woven into *chronos,* the holy invading the ordinary. That's the kind of Christianity that transforms not only a believer's calendar but their consciousness.

Kairos Woven into *Chronos*

The New Testament speaks of time in two distinct ways: *chronos* and *kairos. Chronos* is the ticking of the clock—the ordinary passage of hours and days. *Kairos* is the appointed time—the sacred moment when God breaks into the ordinary. One measures duration; the other measures significance.

When the apostle Paul exhorted believers to "redeem the time" (Ephesians 5:16), he used *kairos*—not to count minutes, but to consecrate moments. To live in Christ is to see every ordinary hour as potential holy ground. The spiritual disciplines become the way we weave *kairos* into *chronos*—the holy invading the ordinary, heaven's rhythm pulsing through daily life.

This is what it means for discipleship to be *infused* rather than merely *scheduled.* Prayer is not a block on the calendar but the breath between tasks. Meditation is not an hour withdrawn but a heart attuned. Witness is not an event but a reflex. Stewardship is not an obligation but a habit of gratitude. When the believer walks in this rhythm, the line between sacred and secular fades;

the presence of God saturates the whole day.

Such Christianity transforms not only a believer's calendar but their consciousness—it redeems time itself, making every hour an opportunity for obedience and every moment a meeting with God.

Conclusion: The Walk that Stands

When the noise of the world fades and the clamor of religion quiets, what remains is the walk of a single believer with God. That is where discipleship is tested — not in the spotlight, but in the silence. The seven disciplines are not rules to keep; they are rhythms to live by. Practiced faithfully, they weave strength into the soul, turning belief into endurance and conviction into peace.

Each discipline carries the same heartbeat: personal followship. Prayer anchors communion, meditation renews the mind, yieldedness bends the will toward obedience. Stewardship teaches responsibility, witness gives faith a voice, gifts-based ministry gives it purpose, and Bible study binds it all together in truth. These are not the habits of the religious few; they are the inheritance of every believer who dares to walk with God when the foundations shake.

No church can practice these on our behalf. No preacher, no program, no public profession can replace the quiet work of the Spirit in a surrendered heart. The church may gather us, but only personal devotion can steady us. The strength of the Body depends upon the faithfulness of its members, and that faithfulness begins when one man or woman decides to follow Christ — alone if necessary, steadfast always.

So let this not be read as a conclusion, but as a commission. Rise each morning with the intent to follow, to pray, to yield, to serve, and to learn. Build your life on what cannot be shaken. When the storm comes — and it surely will — may your heart be found rooted deep in the disciplines that have kept the saints standing through the ages.

This is the call of followship: to walk with Christ day by day, to grow quietly strong, and to become, by His grace, one of those unshaken lives through whom His unshakable Kingdom is made visible.

The Christian warrior who ***trains in peace*** will ***stand in war***. These disciplines are your drills—practice them until they become instinct, so that in the day of battle, obedience moves faster than fear.

Stand-to-Purpose: The Daily March
• Begin each day with one act of surrender and one act of gratitude.
• Practice one discipline intentionally this week until it becomes reflex.
• Journal what obedience cost — and what peace it brought.
• Pray that your private walk becomes your public witness.
• End each day by asking not, "Was I busy?" but, "Was I faithful?"

"Prepare your minds for action; be sober-minded; set your hope fully on the grace that will be brought to you at the revelation of Jesus Christ."

— 1 Peter 1:13

"It is too late to be sparing of preparation and prudent of danger."

— George Washington, 1776

9

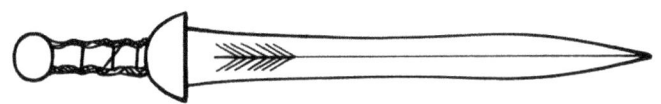

The Trumpet Sounds — Prepare for Battle

"If the trumpet gives an uncertain sound, who shall prepare himself to the battle?"
1 Corinthians 14:8

"Finally, be strong in the Lord and in the strength of His might. Put on the whole armor of God…"
Ephesians 6:10–18

"If you know the enemy and know yourself, you need not fear the result of a hundred battles."
Sun Tzu

Every morning I feel the weight of a heavy brass coin in my pocket. On one side stands a Roman soldier, shield lifted, sword drawn. Around the edge, the inscription reads: **"Put on the Whole Armor of God. Pray Always."** The coin is not a trinket; it is a reminder. It carries the weight of remembrance.

Paul's call to the Ephesians was not poetic suggestion—it was an order from the front. This is not peacetime. The war before the war has already begun. Our generation stands in the midst of cultural, ideological, and spiritual conflict. The trumpet of the Lord is sounding. This is no time for panic, it is a time for preparation.

The War Before the War: Hybrid, Hidden, and Here

Wars are not always fought with bullets. Before the kinetic comes the cultural. Before the gunfire comes the capture of the mind. Long before battlefields erupt, strongholds are built in hearts and institutions. The front line is no longer drawn in trenches but in code; propaganda fits in a pocket and whispers through a screen.

Gramsci designed it as the ***long march through the institutions***. The Frankfurt School refined it into ***cultural critique***. Their disciples dissolved truth into preference and redefined virtue as oppression. Technology scaled their theories, turning digital code into moral code. The result? A slow-motion revolution—a softening of conscience, a seizure of language, and the capture of desire. If we only trace the line back to theorists and tyrants, we stop too soon. The real enemy is older.

Paul warned us: *"We do not wrestle against flesh and blood, but against the rulers, against the authorities, against the cosmic powers over this present darkness."* The devil's playbook has not changed—only his wardrobe. He dresses ideology in reason, tyranny in compassion, and heresy in tolerance.

Reconnaissance: Know the Enemy, Yourself, the Field
1. Know the Enemy

Sun Tzu said, *"If you know the enemy and know yourself, you need not fear the result of a hundred battles."* The enemy of truth today fights on many fronts:

- **Ideological fronts**: cultural Marxism, radical relativism, and the deconstruction of family and faith. They don't burn Bibles; they rewrite them.

- **Political fronts**: authoritarian regimes that criminalize belief and suppress Scripture.
- **Religious fronts**: extremist movements that claim divine sanction for violence, silencing, or domination.
- **Spiritual fronts**: demonic deception that whispers, *"Did God really say?"*

Christians must discern between persons to be loved and powers to be resisted. We fight not against people but against the lies that enslave them.

2. Know Yourself

A church conformed cannot contend. Before we confront the darkness outside, we must repent of the compromise within. The battle for holiness begins at the altar. Leaders must turn from celebrity metrics to biblical ones—from crowds to character, from applause to obedience. We've learned to market the gospel better than we live it. That must end.

3. Know the Field

The terrain of battle is not merely the political arena or the internet feed; it begins at home, extends through the church, and advances into the public square.

- **Home**: the first parish, the first front.
- **Church**: embassy of the Kingdom, a training base for saints.
- **City**: contested ground where schools, councils, and businesses shape minds.
- **Networks**: the new frontiers of formation—media, screens, and systems of meaning.

Field Order: Draw a map of your life's terrain—home, church, city, and network—and mark where truth stands and where compromise has crept in.

The Armor of the Christian
1. The Belt of Truth — Holding It All Together

Roman armor began with the belt. It gathered and secured every other piece of armor. The breastplate, sword, and tunic—anchored to it. Without it, the soldier's protection fell apart. Truth is that belt. Not opinion, not consensus, not "my truth," but the word of God, which anchors every conviction. A Christian soldier without truth is easy prey for propaganda. A preacher without truth becomes a performer.

"Stand therefore, having fastened on the belt of truth." — Ephesians 6:14

Montana Plain: "If your belt's loose, your armor rattles—tighten it with truth."

Truth is not an accessory; it is the structure. Scripture, rightly divided, guards against distortion. Our culture values sincerity over accuracy, but sincerity without truth is self-deception. Believers must anchor convictions to God's word, not the world.

Truth is what holds everything together. Without it, righteousness becomes sentiment, and faith becomes superstition. We must love truth more than comfort and proclaim it without apology. Jesus proclaimed Himself The Way, The Truth, and The Life. And as He faced the cross, He proclaimed that the word of God is truth. In His Priestly Prayer, He stated: *Sanctify them in the truth; your word is truth. As you sent me into the world, so I have sent them into the world. And for their sake I consecrate myself, that they also may be sanctified in truth* (John 17:17-19).

Drill: Memorize three Scriptures that answer the lies most common in your culture.

2. The Breastplate of Righteousness — Guarding the Heart

In battle, the breastplate covered the lungs and heart—the center of breath and life. For the believer, righteousness does the same. This is not self-righteousness; it's the righteousness of Christ imputed to us and expressed through integrity. Sin cracks the plate; hypocrisy corrodes it. Holiness isn't a luxury; it's survival gear.

"Having put on the breastplate of righteousness." — Ephesians 6:14

General George Patton once said, "Moral courage is the most valuable and usually the most absent characteristic in men."

Montana Plain: "Keep the plate solid; a cracked breastplate makes a soft target."

Righteousness is courage under fire—the choice to do right when no one salutes. Paul's metaphor demands inward integrity, not outward pretense. The Roman *cuirass* protected the heart. Righteousness—not self-righteousness but Christ's imputed and imparted life—guards our motives, emotions, and integrity. *"Guard your heart with all diligence,"* Solomon warned, *"for from it flow the springs of life* (Proverbs 4:23)."

Drill: Practice confession. Accountability is armor.

3. The Sandals of the Gospel of Peace — Steady Footing on Shifting Ground

Roman soldiers wore *caligae*, sandals studded with iron cleats to grip the soil. Paul saw in them the readiness that comes from the gospel of peace. The church needs traction again. The gospel gives balance—peace with God that steadies the heart amid chaos, and peace toward others that prevents bitterness from tripping our march.

"Having shod your feet with the preparation of the gospel of peace." — Ephesians 6:15

Montana Plain: "You can't fight long if you keep slipping—peace is your grip."

Peace is not passivity; it is stability—steadiness in conflict. The believer stands firm because Christ's victory is already won. Isaiah foresaw this armor centuries earlier: *"How beautiful upon the mountains are the feet of him who brings good news."* (Isa. 52:7)

As the Roman *caligae* were studded with iron to grip the earth, Christians are to advance, not retreat, rooted in the gospel.

Drill: Take the gospel one step further each week—a conversation, a meal, a prayer.

4. The Shield of Faith — Extinguishing the Arrows

The Roman *scutum* was four feet high, curved, and soaked in water before battle to extinguish flaming darts. Faith does the same for the soul. When the enemy fires lies—*God has abandoned you; you'll never change; you're alone*—the shield of faith intercepts every one. Faith doesn't deny the arrows; it refuses and extinguishes their fire.

"In all circumstances take up the shield of faith, with which you can extinguish all the flaming darts of the evil one." — Ephesians 6:16

Dwight Eisenhower once said, "There are no victories at discount prices." Understand that victory will come at a cost to you.

Montana Plain: "Faith's shield isn't for show—it's for impact."

Roman shields could lock together to form a wall. Faith is communal as much as personal. It quenches the flaming arrows of accusation, doubt, and fear.

Faith forms a wall when believers stand together. It is both personal and corporate defense, forged in trust and tested in battle. *"The righteous shall live by faith."* (Rom. 1:17)

Drill: Join or form a prayer shield. Cover one another's weaknesses.

5. The Helmet of Salvation — Guarding the Mind

A soldier could fight wounded but not decapitated. The helmet protected the critical center of control and vitality. For the believer, salvation guards the mind from despair. When condemnation whispers, *"You're finished,"* the helmet answers, *"It is finished."* Salvation secures the soul's sanity in battle.

"Take the helmet of salvation." — Ephesians 6:17

Montana Plain: "Keep your head in the fight—salvation says who you are when the fog of battle rolls in."

Salvation is more than deliverance from sin; it is the restoration of purpose. The renewed mind resists the propaganda of fear and false identity. The mind is essential, because what captures the mind will eventually command the life. Thus, Paul stresses, *"Be transformed by the renewal of your mind."* (Rom. 12:2)

The mind is the first battlefield. Assurance of salvation guards against despair and propaganda. The helmet fixes our thoughts on eternity.

Drill: Begin each day by declaring your identity: "I am in Christ, and Christ is in me."

6. The Sword of the Spirit — The Word as Weapon

Paul's imagery peaks here. Every prior piece is defensive, but the sword of the Spirit is active, offensive, and alive. It is not the "quotes of the Spirit," but the "sword of the Spirit"—precise Scripture wielded at the moment of need.

"The sword of the Spirit, which is the word of God." — Ephesians 6:17

Montana Plain: "A dull sword's as deadly to the bearer as to the enemy—keep it sharp."

The word of God is not static ink; it is living fire. Hebrews 4:12 declares, *"For the word of God is living and active, sharper than any two-edged sword, piercing to the division of soul and spirit."* Paul wrote to Timothy, *"All Scripture is inspired by God and profitable for teaching, for reproof, for correction, and for training in righteousness."* (2 Tim. 3:16)

This sword is double-edged—it cuts lies from the heart and wounds the darkness itself. But it must be handled rightly. The Spirit wields God's word, and that word reveals the Spirit's mind. Together, they turn disciples into warriors.

The only offensive weapon. The word of God cuts through deception. Jesus Himself wielded it in the wilderness: when Jesus faced Satan in the wilderness, He didn't argue psychology; He unsheathed Scripture: *"It is written."*

Drill: Learn to quote Scripture precisely and apply it timely.

7. Prayer — The Air War

Paul closes his armor list not with silence but with artillery: *"Praying always with all prayer and supplication in the Spirit."* Prayer calls in divine air support. It softens strongholds and opens doors human strategy cannot. Without it, armor becomes costume.

"Pray always with all prayer and supplication in the Spirit." — Ephesians 6:18

Montana Plain: "Armor without prayer is a statue. Looks tough. Doesn't move."

The hymn says, *"Put on the gospel armor, each piece put on with prayer."* Every battle is lost or won before it begins—in the prayer room. The old song *Stand Up, Stand Up for Jesus* captured it perfectly: *"Put on the gospel armor, each piece put on with prayer; where duty calls or danger, be never wanting there."*

To be "wanting" means to be missing. Like Gideon's three hundred, every believer must stand in place, torch raised, trumpet ready. If one soldier is missing, the line breaks. But when every saint stands their ground, the darkness flees.

Prayer isn't a retreat—it's the rally point of heaven's host. Through prayer, we synchronize with the Commander's plan and sustain the fight until victory.

Prayer is the air war—the artillery that precedes and sustains the infantry. *"Praying at all times in the Spirit, with all prayer and supplication."* Prayer keeps the supply lines open.

Drill: Establish a daily rhythm of prayer—adoration, confession, thanksgiving, and supplication. The little acrostic, ACTS, might help you in your engagement in the discipline of prayer.

Montana Plain: "The fire of Pentecost fell on a praying church—and it still does when saints bow."

Truth binds together, righteousness guards, peace steadies, faith shields, salvation anchors, Scripture strikes, and prayer

calls the fire from heaven—together they make a soldier who will not yield.

The armor of God is not ornament and it is not theory—it is the Lord's provision for the hour we are living in. When truth is buckled tight, when righteousness guards the heart, when the Gospel steadies your footing, when faith lifts a shield against the flaming darts, when salvation keeps your mind from collapse, when Scripture is kept sharp, and when prayer keeps you in step with the Commander, you are no longer merely alarmed—you are prepared.

The trumpet is not sounding so we can talk about war; it is sounding so we can stand. And once we are armed, we must be taught how to fight—clean hands, a clear conscience, and holy methods—because the spirit we fight with becomes the spirit we live under.

10

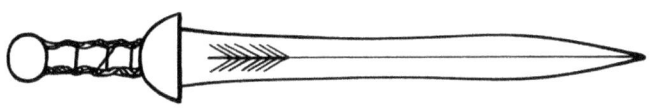

Rules of Engagement
How Christians Contend Without Becoming the Enemy

Every army has rules of engagement; so does Christ's. Ours are not written in Geneva Conventions but in the New Testament. These rules are not restraints meant to weaken us—they are what keep us faithful, clean, and effective in a dirty fight. Without them, zeal turns savage, courage turns cruel, and "truth" becomes an excuse for pride. These disciplines govern our conduct so that conviction remains Christlike even when conflict grows fierce.

This matters because the battle is real—and it is close. But it is not the kind of war most people assume. If we try to win spiritual ground with fleshly weapons, we will inherit fleshly fruit: anger, suspicion, faction, and scorched-earth speech.

The goal is not to "win" arguments and lose souls. The goal is to contend for the faith while keeping the posture of Christ—truth with love, courage with gentleness, purity with restoration, mercy with discernment. The kingdom does not advance through rage; it advances through Spirit-filled people who refuse to bow, refuse to hate, and refuse to lie.

The world knows how to fight dirty; the church must remember how to fight holy.

Truth without malice — The Woman at the Well / The Woman Caught in Adultery (John 4; John 8)

Jesus meets a Samaritan woman at a well and talks about her life plainly (John 4). He doesn't mince doctrine, but he also doesn't throw the first stone.

Later in His ministry, a woman is dragged before him charged with adultery—caught in the very act. The accusers want spectacle and ruin—not just of the woman but of Jesus. Jesus wants repentance and restoration (John 8).

The accusers quoted the Scripture—those caught in adultery, must be stoned. "What say you, master?" they demanded. Much speculation has gone into what Jesus wrote on the ground. Given their appeal to the law, He might simply have written one damning question: "Where's the man?"

He exposed the hypocrisy of her judges, and gave the woman a future (*"Go and sin no more"*), and refused to humiliate her. The line is clear: truth was spoken, false judgment exposed, and a path back opened. He told the truth *and* let grace do its work.

"Rather, speaking the truth in love, we are to grow up in every way into him who is the head, into Christ (Ephesians 4:15)."

Speak the truth, but let love be the frame. Truth that wounds for the sake of wounding becomes gossip; truth delivered in love convicts and heals. Practice precision: name the falsehood, state the evidence, point to the gospel alternative—and stop. Don't drag character assassination into doctrinal correction. The aim is restoration, not revenge; the aim is to expose the lie so a person can be set free, not humiliated into retreat.

Application: Name the sin; refuse the mob-trial; offer a route to repentance. Say what is true — but say it so the person can return, not so they'll be ruined.

Sermon seed: Tell the truth—but keep your stones on the ground.

Courage without Contempt: Paul at the Areopagus

Paul stands before a skeptical culture in Athens. His team of fellow missionaries have not yet arrived. The zealous Paul could take the silence no longer. Standing before marble idols, alone but unashamed, he began to engage the philosophers of Athens on Mars Hill (Acts 17).

He didn't mock their ignorance; he built a bridge of understanding—*"What you worship as unknown, I proclaim to you."* That is courage baptized in respect. He does not sneer. He listens, quotes their poets, and then names the true God plainly.

That is courage: confronting error in the public square — but done in a way that invites thought rather than triggering reflexive rage. Paul's posture opens doors (some mocked, some believed). Courage need not be contemptuous; it can be winsome and direct at once.

> *But in your hearts honor Christ the Lord as holy, always being prepared to make a defense to anyone who asks you for a reason for the hope that is in you; yet do it with gentleness and respect.*
> (1 Peter 3:15)

Be brave enough to say what must be said and gentle enough to keep a hand on the shoulder when you say it. Courage that descends into contempt closes ears and hardens hearts; it turns prophetic witness into public flogging. Learn to distinguish firmness from fury. Stand firm on truth, but welcome questions; steel your convictions and soften your delivery. Remember: an insult wins the argument for no one and destroys the chance of a future conversation.

Application: Be bold in the marketplace of ideas; do not weaponize scorn. Courage that wins converts; contempt wins converts to contempt. Boldness must never become bitterness.

Sermon seed: Courage doesn't sneer; it speaks steady truth in hostile places.

Purity without Prudishness — Corinth's Discipline and Restoration

When the Corinthian church tolerated a public, scandalous sin, Paul ordered decisive discipline — remove the offender so the church's witness remains intact (1 Cor. 5:1-7). That discipline was not vindictive, it was necessary for the health of the infant church.

Later, in his second epistle to the Corinthians, Paul urges the church to forgive and restore the repentant brother *"so that he will not be overwhelmed by excessive sorrow"* (2 Cor. 2:7–11). The two acts — firm boundary and tender restoration — belong together: holiness enforced, restoration offered. Purity that becomes a courtroom without a hospital is cruel; purity that becomes a club without boundaries destroys witness.

"Let marriage be held in honor among all, and let the marriage bed be undefiled, for God will judge the sexually immoral and adulterous (Hebrews 13:4)."

Hold sexual holiness high without turning tenderness into a tribunal. Purity protects the vulnerable and honors the covenant; prudishness judges and alienates the broken. Here's what we can learn from the way Paul dealt with the situation in Corinth:

- Name sin plainly, but also name grace more plainly.

- Address sin—all sin--openly and with both force and grace. (The sexual sin used as an example is merely representative of all our rebellion against God. But the way Paul dealt with the sin is exemplary.)
- Offer correction with pathways back—repentance, accountability, pastoral care—so people aren't shoved out the door but led home.

The church must be both a hospital for sinners and a refinery for saints.

Application: Protect the body by drawing firm lines; when repentance comes, lead the way in restoration. The holy are not the haughty.

Sermon seed: Guard the gate and keep a hand outstretched to the prodigal coming home.

Mercy without Muddle — The Prodigal Son and the Running Father
How fast does mercy move?

In Jesus' parable of the lost son in Luke 15, ***it runs***.

The younger son squandered his inheritance. Broken and ashamed, he vowed to return. The father did not wait for a perfect apology — seeing the son coming home, the father runs, embraces, restores, and feasts. The father sprints toward the son—but he doesn't rewrite the past. Mercy meets truth at the embrace. Mercy is lavish—robes, ring, fatted calf.

But mercy here is not sloppy: it reconvenes the family covenant and insists on repentance's fruit. Mercy that ignores the damage done or refuses reconciliation ends in chaos; mercy that insists on reconciliation heals.

"And have mercy on those who doubt; save others by snatching them out of the fire; to others show mercy with fear, hating even the garment stained by the flesh (Jude 22-23)."

Compassion is not ambiguity. Mercy rescues, compassion disciplines toward health, and grace confronts falsehood that would harm others. To be merciful without clarity is to leave corruption unchallenged; to be clear without mercy is to wound.

Walk both lanes: reach out to the sinner with patient love while refusing to normalize patterns that destroy. Mercy that lacks boundaries becomes an enabling force; mercy that knows limits becomes liberating to those trapped by sin.

Application: Give extravagant grace, but insist on the hard work of repentance and reconciliation afterward.

Sermon seed: Mercy runs to restore. It runs faster than gossip and farther than shame.

Zeal without Zealotry — Paul Rebukes Peter at Antioch

Picture the tension in Antioch: two apostles face to face. Paul's voice trembles, not with rage but with grief—because compromise threatens the gospel. Zeal defended the truth without devouring a brother.

When Peter began to withdraw from table fellowship out of fear of certain Jews, Paul publicly confronted him (Gal. 2:11-14). Paul's zeal for the gospel led him to rebuke a fellow apostle — not to tear down a brother but to protect the gospel's truth: the gospel is for Jew and Gentile alike. That episode shows fierce conviction shaped by gospel priorities, not factional fury. Zeal must be tethered to the gospel, not to a party line or personality cult. If Christ isn't the center of your passion, pride soon will be.

"For I bear them witness that they have a zeal for God, but not according to knowledge. For, being ignorant of the righteousness of God, and seeking to establish their own, they did not submit to God's righteousness. For Christ is the end of the law for righteousness to everyone who believes (Rom. 10:2-4)."

Be passionate for the truth without mistaking passion for perfection. Zeal fires the furnace of obedience; zealotry turns that furnace on neighbors. Anchor your zeal in Scripture, not in slogans or factional loyalties. Test your movements: do they draw people toward Christ or toward your faction? If the answer is the latter, reorient. Humble zeal asks better questions, not just louder ones.

Application: Fight hard for what the gospel requires; refuse to turn zeal into exclusionary tribalism.

Sermon seed: Let zeal guard the gospel, not your ego. Passion must stay yoked to humility.

Patience without Passivity — Barnabas and the Long Game

When the church in Jerusalem feared Paul after his conversion, Barnabas stepped in: he vouched for Paul (Acts 9), mentored him, and later helped gather a new, flourishing church in Antioch (Acts 11:19-26). Barnabas's patience was active — he trained leaders, bore risk, and stayed in the work when quick wins were scarce. He played the long game.

Patience here is a strategy: steady discipling, persistent pastoral work, and consistent obedience. All goal-focused. His reward was more than a nickname—it was a strong, missional church in Antioch and the gospel spreading throughout the Roman Empire. His grace and patience shaped a missionary movement. Passive men wait for safe odds; patient men invest early.

Bide your time, but train while you wait. Patience is strength under restraint—steadfast endurance that plans, prepares, and gently persuades. Passivity, by contrast, shrugs and hopes everything will fix itself. Keep working: mend relationships, disciple new leaders, restore denominational wounds, and build institutions of faithfulness. Pray with urgency; act with consistency.

The kingdom advances through men and women who refuse to quit, even when applause fades and headlines mock. The patient saints always outlast the storm.

Application: Wait, yes — but work while you wait. Patience builds powerful saints, mentors leaders, and keeps the line intact.

Sermon seed: Patience works while it waits. We wait, but we do not withdraw.

Order without Ossification — "The Council That Saved the Church"

In Jerusalem, a packed hall was filled with hot debate. The future of the gospel for Gentiles hung in the balance. Faced with a divisive question (must Gentiles be circumcised?), the early church did not side-step the issue. The Council gathered, debated, tested Scripture, listened to Spirit-formed testimony, then issued a clear, flexible ruling suited to mission (Acts 15).

The Council created structure that served mission rather than preserved previous custom for its own sake. While order mattered; rigid rule-making that chokes mission did not. What that first church Council decided set the stage for the gospel to go global…just as Jesus commanded.

The apostles choose process over panic, Scripture over slogans, and mission over custom. The way they faced this divisive issue became a channel for grace, not a cage.

Structure gives longevity while rigidity kills vitality. Create clear practices—disciplines of prayer, instruction, witness, and care—that sustain a faithful people across seasons. But refuse traditions that calcify into idols. When form serves life, keep it. But when form chokes life, reform it or reject it. Ecclesial order must protect truth and enable mission, not preserve nostalgia.

Application: At the local church level, cultivate leadership that listens—to Scripture, to the Spirit, and to faithful testimony. Order your congregation for mission, not maintenance. Practices that sustain prayer, teaching, care, and witness should be strengthened; traditions that exist only because "we've always done it this way" should be tested. Healthy churches reform their structures before those structures fossilize their calling.

Sermon seed:
Structure should be strong enough to hold the truth and supple enough for the Spirit to move the church outward in mission. Keep structures flexible so the Spirit can breathe through them.

Remember: *the spirit you fight with becomes the spirit you live under.* If we war in the flesh, we will inherit its fruit—anger, suspicion, pride. If we fight in the Spirit, we will bear His fruit—love, joy, peace.

The Battle Plan: Jude 20–23

Jude opens his brief but blazing epistle with a command to *"contend for the faith that was once for all delivered to the saints."* He identifies enemies already inside the camp—those who *"pervert the grace of our God into sensuality and deny our only Master and Lord, Jesus Christ,"* who *"defile the flesh, reject authority, and blaspheme."* He leaves no ambiguity: they are marked for judgment. The Lord Himself will come *"to execute judgment on all and to convict all the ungodly"* for their deeds and their defiance.

Jude sketches them in plain lines so we cannot mistake them: *"grumblers, malcontents, following their own sinful desires; loud-mouthed boasters, showing favoritism to gain advantage."*

Against this internal sabotage, Jude does not tell the church to panic or hide; he gives a battle plan. *"But you, beloved,"* he writes, *"build yourselves up in your most holy faith; pray in the Holy Spirit; keep yourselves in the love of God; wait for the mercy of our Lord Jesus Christ… have mercy on those who doubt; save others by snatching them out of the fire…"* (Jude 20–23).

Jude's battle plan for believers unfolds in six movements:

1. Build Up — Train your people in doctrine and truth. Spiritual flimsy comes from doctrinal famine. To *"build yourselves up"* is to fortify minds and hearts with the whole counsel of God so that counterfeits are immediately recognized. A church that is well-fed on Scripture is hard to fool and harder to move.

When the pastor-teachers are doing what the church needs—equipping the saints for their work of ministry, spiritual maturity will result. Listen to what Paul says in Ephesians 4:13-16:

Until we all attain to the unity of the faith and of the knowledge of the Son of God, to mature manhood, to the measure of the stature of the fullness of Christ, ***so that we may no longer be children, tossed to and fro by the waves and carried about by every wind of doctrine, by human cunning, by craftiness in deceitful schemes****. Rather, speaking the truth in love, we are to grow up in every way into him who is the head, into Christ, from whom the whole body, joined and held together by every joint with which it is equipped, when each part is working properly, makes the body grow so that it builds itself up in love.*

And if our leaders won't, then we must. We exercise ourselves in the disciplines of the faith. We commit to do the necessary work like the athlete who hits the gym—not to watch, but to be shaped by steel.

2. Pray — Establish intercessory networks; the prayer meeting is the war room. *"Praying in the Holy Spirit"* is not ornamental language; it is operational necessity. When he commands that we pray in the Spirit, we recognize that at our very best, our prayers miss the mark.

But again the Apostle Paul, the great explainer, helps our understanding: *Likewise the Spirit helps us in our weakness. For we do not know what to pray for as we ought, but the Spirit himself intercedes for us with groanings too deep for words. And he who searches hearts knows what is the mind of the Spirit, because the Spirit intercedes for the saints according to the will of God* (Rom. 8:26-27).

When we pray in the Spirit we are aligning our will with the will of the Father. The Spirit of God who indwells us aligns our will with God's, opens doors no human strategy can open, and holds ground no man-made program can hold.

When intercession wanes, infiltration wins. Hell never sleeps—why should our prayer life?

3. Keep — Maintain unity and holiness within the camp.
"*Keep yourselves in the love of God*" means remain in the sphere where His love rules: obedient, repentant, reconciled. Jesus gave us an indication of Jude's directive: *As the Father has loved me, so have I loved you. Abide in my love. If you keep my commandments, you will abide in my love, just as I have kept my Father's commandments and abide in his love* (John 15:9-10). Obedience is the key to abiding. Obedience to the Father's commandments will guard the fellowship from bitterness, division, and quiet rebellion. A fractured, resentful church is already half-defeated.

4. Wait — Develop endurance; God's timing wins wars.
"*Waiting for the mercy of our Lord Jesus Christ*" fixes our hope forward. We do not lunge in panic or quit in fatigue; we endure with eyes lifted to the appearing of Christ. We live in the expectation of the coming of Christ and the fullness of our salvation and the ultimate deliverance from evil. *Waiting* here is not laziness; it is loyal perseverance under fire, trusting that final vindication is His to give.

5. Have Mercy — Rescue the wavering; the battle is for souls.
"*Have mercy on those who doubt*" assumes that some in the ranks will be shaken. We do not shoot the wounded; we steady them. Answer honest questions, walk patiently with the unsure, and treat doubters as people to be rescued, not traitors to be discarded.

6. Save — Go after the lost; snatch them from the fire. "*Save others by snatching them out of the fire*" is combat language. We move toward those in grave spiritual danger with urgency and clarity, hating the sin that clings to them but refusing to abandon them to it. The mission is not maintenance; it is rescue—close-quarters, costly, deliberate.

We take the message of the forgiveness of God that is ours in Christ to the world we enter every day. ***As we are going***, we are to be His witnesses—the proclaimers of good news.

In the commission Jesus gave to the disciples at the end of Luke's gospel, we find our marching orders: *"These are my words that I spoke to you while I was still with you, that everything written about me in the Law of Moses and the Prophets and the Psalms must be fulfilled." Then he opened their minds to understand the Scriptures, and said to them, "Thus it is written, that the Christ should suffer and on the third day rise from the dead, and that repentance for the forgiveness of sins should be proclaimed in his name to all nations, beginning from Jerusalem. You are witnesses of these things* (Luke 24:44-48).

Witness is not just what we do, it is who we are.

Operational Order: Build → Pray → Keep → Wait → Show Mercy → Save.

This is how a remnant holds the line without losing its heart.

Standing Orders for the Saints

We fight not as crusaders of wrath but as ambassadors of reconciliation. The armory is open and the orders are clear. The belt of truth is buckled; the breastplate shines with righteousness; the shield still bears the scorch marks of battle but holds fast. The sword has been tested. The helmet fits snug against fear. The sandals grip steady ground.

We are not called to admire the armor but to wear it. Not to sing about the battle but to enter it. Not to curse the darkness but to pierce it with light.

The war will not wait for our convenience. It will meet us in our homes, in our pulpits, in our schools, and in our cities. It will test our integrity and tempt our silence. But the soldier of Christ does not retreat—he stands.

Our orders are holy, and so must our methods be:
- Truth without malice.
- Courage without contempt.
- Purity without prudishness.
- Mercy without muddle.
- Zeal without zealotry.
- Patience without passivity.
- Order without ossification.

These are not suggestions. They are standing orders for saints not to bow to the spirit of the age.

We are a people armed by grace, governed by love, and steadied by hope. Every flicker of faith is a flare that signals heaven's resistance. Our Captain has gone before us, and His banner still flies over the field. We march beneath that banner until the day the trumpet sounds again—not to prepare for battle, but to signal its end.

Montana Plain: "Until then—keep your armor close, your heart clean, and your head up. The war's not over, but neither is our Commander."

Benediction: The Trumpet Hour

Captain of our Salvation,
Steady our hands and strengthen our hearts.
Gird us with truth, fit us with righteousness.
Crown our minds with salvation.
Teach our hands for war and our hearts for worship.

Make us gentle with the broken and fierce with the devourer.
Form shepherd-warriors, household altars, and congregations that sing in the night.
Until the last trumpet sounds, may our armor never gather dust.
Until the darkness breaks and the nations confess,
May we be found standing—armored, faithful, and unafraid.
Amen.

Church Readiness Assessment

On page 207 in the Appendix, you will find a **Church Readiness Assessment**. It is designed to assist pastors, leaders, and believers in evaluating whether their ministries and lives are aligned with the mission of Christ or have drifted toward the values of the world.

Note:

We have defined the armor and the battle. Now we must be crystal clear about the kind of battle this is not.

Interlude — *Christian Nonviolence and the Nature of the Christian Battle*

"That's Enough"
Why Jesus Mentioned Two Swords—And What It *Doesn't* Mean

The Text and the Tension
Late in Passion Week, with the shadow of the cross stretching across Jerusalem, Jesus asked His disciples: *"How many swords do you have?"* They answered, *"Two."* And Jesus said, *"That's enough."* — Luke 22:36–38

Across church history, this exchange has been **misread, abused, allegorized, weaponized, and misunderstood**. Some critics of Christianity wield it as a proof text that Jesus endorsed violence. Some fringe movements use it to justify armed resistance. Some theologians—embarrassed by the literal reading—allegorize the swords into metaphors for Scripture and faith.

Yet the context of the ancient world, the nature of Roman law, and Jesus' own actions make clear what this moment actually means. This passage is not about violence. Not about self-defense.

And certainly not about insurrection. It is about the **legal optics** required to classify Jesus and His disciples as transgressors under Roman authority—*and the prophetic necessity* that the Messiah be *"numbered with the transgressors."*

The Roman Legal Environment: Why Two Swords Mattered
In the first century, Judea was a powder keg. Armed groups—

often small—were routinely labeled:
- *lēstai* (bandits, insurgents, rebels)
- *stasiastai* (agitators, seditionists)

Rome did not distinguish between a political cell, a band of robbers, or a small nationalist group. If a leader had followers—and those followers carried **even minimal weaponry**—they could be treated as a revolutionary faction.

Two swords were not enough to fight Rome. Any uprising that had only two swords was a suicide squad. But two swords were enough—enough to **classify** a group under Roman law as potentially subversive.

This is crucial: Jesus' arrest, trial, and execution all hinge on **Rome treating Him as a political threat**. His crucifixion was not for blasphemy (Rome didn't care). It was for sedition—the crime of a rebel king. That's why the placard above His head read:

"Jesus of Nazareth, King of the Jews"

That declaration was true in its full spiritual and prophetic sense. But it also reflected the necessary charge that Pilate needed to conduct what was determined before there was ever a Roman Empire—the crucifixion of Jesus as the Lamb of God who would bear the sins of the whole world.

Why Jesus Asked About the Swords

Jesus wasn't taking inventory for self-defense. He was declaring that prophecy and politics were converging in a single moment.

Two swords fulfilled two conditions:
A. Prophetic: *"He was numbered among the transgressors."*
Isaiah foresaw the Servant counted as a criminal. To be

"numbered" meant seen, treated, and charged as one.

B. Legal: Rome needed justification.
A teacher with unarmed disciples is merely eccentric. A teacher with **armed** disciples can be crucified as a threat to the State.

Jesus' words, "*That's enough*," mean: **The requirement is satisfied. Nothing more is needed.** He wasn't saying, "Two swords are enough for a fight." He was saying, "Two swords are enough for what must unfold."

Jesus' Own Actions Make the Meaning Clear
Later that evening, the mob came to arrest Jesus and the disciples. They probably came first to the place where Judas had last seen them—the upper room. When they were not found there, Judas led them on to the favorite place where Jesus retreated for prayer—the Garden of Gethsemane.

If Jesus intended violence, the moment Judas kissed Him on His cheek to identify which man the mob needed to apprehend—that was the time for the fight to begin. But the response of Jesus laid that charge of rebellion to rest.
- Why tell Peter to put away the sword?
- Why heal the man Peter wounded?
- Why forbid resistance?
- Why tell Pilate His kingdom is not advanced by fighting?
- Why willingly submit to arrest?

Jesus nullifies every violent interpretation by His own behavior. Peter's sword stroke is not a sanctioned act of defense; it is a **failure to understand the mission.**

Jesus could not have rebuked violence more swiftly or more clearly.

Allegorical Readings Miss the Point

Some Christian interpreters throughout history—embarrassed by the literal verbs—recast the two swords as symbols. They use a form of interpretation called the allegorical method. That method essentially allows the interpreter to layer any meaning they want on the text. Here's what they have mistakenly stated:

- "The spiritual sword of Scripture."
- "The sword of faith and the sword of doctrine."
- "The two spheres of church and state."

But these readings collapse under textual, historical, and narrative scrutiny:

- The disciples responded with literal weapons.
- Jesus' rebuke of Peter's sword only makes sense if the swords were literal.
- The Temple guards later arrest Jesus *on grounds appropriate to armed men.*

Allegory washes the text clean of its actual geopolitical and legal context.

This is not a parable. It is a courtroom set-up. A prophetic staging. A legal qualification for crucifixion that was in the sphere of Pilate's authority as the Roman Empire's representative.

Why This Passage Does *Not* Justify Christian Violence

To claim Jesus sanctioned violence because two disciples carried swords is:

- **a misunderstanding of Roman law**,
- **a misreading of the narrative**, and
- **a rejection of Jesus' explicit teaching.**

Jesus never says, "Use them."
He never says, "Defend me."
He never says, "Fight the State."
He says, *"That's enough"*—not for battle, but for **classification**.

What follows is pure nonviolence:
- He surrenders.
- He forbids fighting.
- He heals His enemy.
- He rebukes violence as contrary to His kingdom.

The real "battle" of the two swords passage is the war **for the soul**, not the state. It is the war **against lies**, not against Rome. It is the war **against darkness**, not against flesh and blood.

The Christian Battle: Spiritual, Not Physical

This is where this essay supports the larger argument in *Called to Stand*.
- **We fight principalities, not police.**
- **We resist ideologies, not individuals.**
- **We wage war through prayer, truth, formation, courage, and proclamation—not through force.**

Jesus used two swords to walk into the machinery of Rome, not to establish a Christian militia. The early church—persecuted, unarmed, unprotected—won the empire not with steel, but with steadfastness.

Why This Matters Today

In a world where Christians are often caricatured as politically militant or culturally hostile, we must be crystal clear:

Christian courage is not Christian violence.

Christian warfare is not physical warfare.
Christian resistance is spiritual, moral, and prophetic— not militaristic.

Luke 22 does not call the church to arms. It calls the church to **clarity, integrity, and readiness for persecution**, not readiness for insurrection. Jesus' two swords were not for battle. They were for a trial. And the trial led to a cross. And the cross led to a kingdom not built by force, but by the power of God.

The "two swords" passage is not a loophole for Christian violence. It is the moment Jesus steps decisively into His identity as the suffering Messiah—treated as a transgressor, condemned as a rebel, yet conquering not by the sword, but by the sacrifice. The cross, not coercion, is the victory of God.

And for His followers, the only battlefield that matters is the one **within the soul and within the culture**, not upon the streets.

The Battlefields We Cannot Abandon

Jesus never called His disciples to take up arms against Rome. Two swords were not a call for insurrection; they were a rebuke to misdirected zeal. But neither was the Kingdom of God an invitation to political withdrawal.

The New Testament does not present government as an enemy to escape but as an arena in which righteousness, justice, and truth are meant to be visible through God's people. Paul appealed to Roman citizenship. Peter instructed believers to honor the king. The apostles preached in public forums, reasoned in synagogues, confronted idolatry in city centers, and defended the faith before magistrates and governors.

The Kingdom of God is not of this world — but its citizens are still in this world, responsible for what happens on the ground where God has placed them.

A Republic Demands Its Citizens

America is not an empire ruled by decree. It is not a monarchy ruled by lineage. It is a constitutional republic — a nation whose power flows, in theory and in structure, from the consent of the governed.

In such a system, silence is not neutrality; it is abdication. When citizens are granted the privilege of representation, they bear the responsibility of participation.

If the church withdraws from civic life, it does not create a vacuum of neutrality — it creates a vacancy that will be filled by competing worldviews, many of which openly oppose biblical truth, human dignity, and ordered liberty.

The Christian who refuses to engage in public life is not practicing humility. He is surrendering stewardship.

The Public Square Is Not Off-Limits

For too long, the church has treated civic engagement as contamination rather than calling.

Out of fear of partisanship, Christians abandoned the field.

Out of fear of offense, pulpits fell silent on moral clarity.

Out of fear of misinterpretation, believers retreated to private devotion while public institutions were reshaped by ideologies hostile to truth.

But moral issues do not cease to be moral when they enter the legislature. Cultural questions do not cease to be spiritual when they enter the classroom. Political decisions do not cease to be theological when they redefine marriage, life, justice, or freedom.

The fields of battle include families, schools, universities, pulpits, media, and the machinery of government itself. Everywhere conscience is shaped, culture is formed, and law is written — those places are battlegrounds.

Not for violence.
Not for vengeance.
But for voice.

Advocacy Is Not Insurrection; It Is Obedience

To vote is not to seize Caesar's sword; it is to steward Caesar's office. To speak in the public square is not to confuse church and state; it is to resist the silencing of conscience. To elect leaders who uphold moral order is not to idolize politics; it is to obey the command to *"seek the welfare of the city"* (Jer. 29:7).

Christians are not called to overthrow the republic — they are called to uphold it. A constitutional republic cannot survive without a moral people. Hear the voice of John Adams:

"Our Constitution was made only for a moral and religious people. It is wholly inadequate to the government of any other."

— to the Officers of the First Brigade of the Third Division of the Militia of Massachusetts, 1798

This is not "Christian nationalism" or a theocratic impulse. Adams isn't calling for clerical rule—he's warning about moral vacuum. If believers leave the shaping of law and culture to those who reject the foundations on which the republic stands, then the republic will not stand much longer.

Engagement Without Enmity

Our weapons are not swords but Scripture. Not militancy but mercy. Not coercion but conviction.

We do not wage war as the world wages war. But we do engage. We advocate. We speak. We vote. We disciple our families, strengthen our churches, equip our young, and contend for truth in the marketplace of ideas.

To disengage from public life is not a mark of holiness — it is a symptom of defeat.

Christians Are Custodians of Conscience

In every era, God calls His people to stand in the public square as custodians of conscience.

- Not to impose faith by force, but to illuminate truth by presence.
- Not to demand privilege, but to defend the dignity of all people.
- Not to secure comfort, but to uphold righteousness.

When Christians stand absent, the culture will not remain neutral — it will be discipled by those who deny the very truths that make freedom possible.

This Is Not a Call to Arms — It Is a Call to Awake

We reject the sword of revolution. We embrace the plowshare of responsibility.

We reject the fury of mobs. We embrace the steady courage of faithful citizenship.

We stand not as insurgents but as intercessors, not as conquerors but as caretakers, not as partisans but as witnesses, not for power but for truth.

If America is to endure, the church cannot merely pray for renewal — it must participate in it.

Not with violence. Not with vengeance. But with virtue, vigilance, and a voice that refuses to bow to the spirit of the age.

Christians do not seek to rule the nation. But we dare not refuse the responsibility to shape it. For in a republic, discipleship and citizenship are inseparable; and in a collapsing culture, silence is complicity.

11

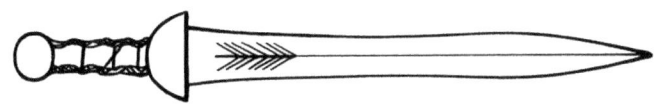

When God Rends the Heavens

"Oh, that You would rend the heavens and come down…"
Isaiah 64:1

There are hours in history when nations tremble, when the ground under their feet shifts, and when the quiet sins of a people erupt into loud consequences. Those hours are judgment, and mercy, and invitation all at once. America now stands in such an hour.

Our idols have failed us.
Our institutions splinter.
Our children stagger beneath confusion.
Our leaders grasp for power without principle.
Our churches — too many of them — have grown fluent in comfort and mute in conviction.

And yet this, strangely, is the very kind of soil God has always plowed before awakening. Before He visits with power, He permits shaking — so that men may remember they are dust, nations may feel their frailty, the church may recall she is not a brand but a Bride, and shepherds may realize they are not entertainers but watchmen. When shaking turns to seeking, mercy is never far behind.

> *"Will You not revive us again, that Your people may rejoice in You?"* — Psalm 85:6

We stand at the hinge of history. The trumpet of the Lord sounds — not for retreat, but for repentance, readiness, and resolve. It is time to set our faces like flint and prepare the altars for fire.

Disciplined Lives — Awakened Nations

Across centuries and continents revival has not sprung from whim or hype, but from men and women who practiced the disciplines long before the trumpet sounded. It is a reminder to us: The disciplines you practice in your quiet hour today may well be the seedbed of your nation's coming awakening tomorrow.

"We do not study revival to admire the past, but to recognize the same God who still walks our streets in unseen splendor."

Look at a few movements of God in just the last few centuries in which God shook the foundations.

Martin Luther — The Word That Shook the World

Before there was thunder in Wittenberg, there was silence in a monk's cell.

Martin Luther had worn his knees raw on the cold stones of the monastery floor, confessing every sin he could remember and inventing more to appease a conscience that would not rest. His was a life of discipline without peace—fasting, study, prayer, penance—all without assurance that God could truly love him.

Then one night, while lecturing through *Romans*, the light

broke. He came to the words: *"The righteous shall live by faith"* (Romans 1:17).

In that instant the Scriptures ceased to be a wall of judgment and became a door of grace. Luther later wrote, "I felt myself to be reborn and to have gone through open doors into paradise."

His chains broke and the Reformation began. That revelation from inspired text illuminated by the Spirit of God ignited a restoration of New Testament faith. What began as a monk's encounter with one verse became a movement that reshaped nations. The hammer blows that echoed from Wittenberg's door were the sound of truth breaking chains forged by centuries of superstition.

Revival, it turns out, does not begin in crowds—it begins in the solitude of a searching heart disciplined to wrestle with the word of God.

Montana Plain: "When one man's knees hit the floor, the world sometimes shakes."

The First Great Awakening — Truth in Flames.
In the 18th-century Oxford of John and Charles Wesley, a young student by the name of George Whitefield joined the Holy Club and adopted a regimen of prayer, Scripture, fasting, and accountability. From that discipline came the open-air revivals that changed Britain and America.

Whitefield thundered and Edwards wept. Sin was exposed, Christ exalted, and a sleeping church remembered it had a soul.

The Second Great Awakening — Repentance in Motion.
Frontiers shook with camp meetings and Wesleyan fire that spread through cabins, fields, and schoolhouses. Farmers, soldiers, mothers, and statesmen knelt together, and the moral compass of a nation reset.

The Prayer Revival of 1857 — Ordinary Saints, Extraordinary God.

There were no celebrities, no promotions, no lights — just lunchtime prayer meetings in New York that spread like wildfire. Men prayed; heaven bent low. On the brink of civil war, God steadied a nation.

Azusa Street — Fire in a Warehouse

Five decades later, a different kind of thunder rolled through Los Angeles.

The year was 1906. The world was changing—industry rising, cities sprawling, hearts cooling. But in a little mission on Azusa Street, a one-eyed Black preacher named **William J. Seymour** gathered a handful of believers who refused to accept a powerless church. What became known as the Azusa Street revival surged not from a sensational preacher, but from months of humble prayer, fasting, and worship in a run-down mission. From discipline flowed explosion.

They prayed day and night in a drafty room with wooden crates for pews. No budget, no publicity—just hunger. The sermons were simple, the floorboards dusty, and the atmosphere thick with repentance and expectancy. Then, as eyewitnesses recorded, "the heavens opened." People wept, confessed sins, spoke reconciliation, and sang until dawn. Race, class, and gender distinctions melted in the presence of God.

From that forgotten street corner, the Pentecostal movement spread to every continent, carrying the gospel in more languages than any missionary board could plan.

The power that fell at Azusa did not descend on celebrity, but on obedience. These men and women had stacked the wood of prayer and humility; God lit the fire.

Montana Plain: "When prayer replaces pride, heaven finds an address."

The Korean Prayer Revival — Fire on the Hills (1907)

The winter of 1907 found Pyongyang—then called "the Jerusalem of the East"—covered in snow and silence. Korea was humiliated politically, fractured spiritually, and overshadowed by foreign control. Yet in that bleak season, a handful of missionaries and Korean elders gathered for a Bible conference and prayer. They began to confess their sins—jealousy, resentment, unbelief—and the room broke open. Weeping turned to worship, and conviction to cleansing.

What began in one small church spread across the nation. Businesses closed so owners could attend prayer meetings. Thieves returned stolen goods. Families reconciled. The Spirit of God swept through the country like wind over dry grass.

Out of that movement came a culture of prayer that still marks the Korean church today—*dawn prayers before sunrise, fasting chains, all-night vigils, mountain retreats where prayer sounds like thunder rolling through the valleys.*

A century later, that flame still burns. In 1973, a million people filled Yoido Plaza in Seoul to hear evangelist Billy Graham—the largest single gathering of believers in modern history. The world's largest church, Yoido Full Gospel Church, rose from those same roots—built not on spectacle but on the prayer culture birthed in that revival. That culture found expression in home cells, prayer mountains, and disciplined faith that never forgot the lesson of 1907: when God's people pray, heaven bends low.

Montana Plain: "When prayer climbs the mountain before dawn, power follows with the daylight."

The Hebrides Revival — When Two Sisters Prayed (1949–1952)

Far to the west, on the wind-scoured islands of Scotland, two elderly sisters—Peggy and Christine Smith, one blind, the other bent with arthritis—could no longer attend church. So they turned their cottage into an altar. Night after night, they prayed Isaiah 44:3: *"I will pour water on the thirsty land and streams on the dry ground."*

Their pastor, stirred by their faith, called the men of the parish to prayer in a barn. For months they wrestled heavenward until one night the floor itself seemed to tremble. The Spirit of God swept through the Hebrides. Fishermen fell to their knees on their boats; people awoke in the middle of the night under conviction and ran to churches that had no scheduled meetings.

Duncan Campbell, the evangelist later called to the island, said, "The community was saturated with God."

There were no programs, no advertisements—only holiness breaking through human habit. The revival burned quietly but deeply, leaving behind a purified church and a humbled people.

Montana Plain: "When saints who cannot stand still pray, whole islands bow low."

The Pattern of Heaven — What God Honors

Across centuries and continents, the soil of awakening softens in the same way.

First comes holy dissatisfaction — that restless awareness that religion without presence is not enough. People grow weary of programs without power and sermons without surrender.

Then humility and repentance. God has never visited a prideful church. Not the legal kind of repentance, not the public-relations kind — but heart-crushed, altar-soaked repentance that breaks the hardness of the soul. From the monk's cell to the mountain church, the pattern remains: humility kindles holiness; prayer precedes power.

Then comes prevailing prayer. Not polite or efficient prayer, but the kind that weeps and wrestles — midnight prayer, *"groanings too deep for words."* Every awakening is born on its knees, not on a platform.

Then the fear of the Lord. Not terror, but trembling wonder — the hush where sin feels heavy and God feels near, where no one dares to mock because no one can speak at all.

Then Scripture with fire. Doctrine falls like dew, truth thunders, and the pulpit stops whispering. The word of God becomes a sword in the marrow — warning, weeping, awakening.

Then youth ignited. God delights to place torches in young hands, saving them from despair and sending them running with His Name on their lips.

And finally, **evangelism without effort.** When God rends the heavens, lost people find the door without invitation. They wake under conviction, knock before sunrise, and tremble in fields and factories. Revival is not when the church grows louder — it is when God speaks and the world hears.

And through the years He did it again and again: Wales with its songs of holiness, Azusa Street with its global evangelism, the Hebrides where two elderly sisters prayed and an island shook, the Jesus Movement that baptized hippies by the thousands,

Brownsville and Asbury where repentance and worship flowed in tears.

Different lands, different vessels — the same God. Heaven bent. Earth shook. Souls burned bright.

Coda: The Unbroken Pattern
From Oxford's halls to New England's pulpits, from frontier Kentucky to the prayer halls of New York, from Pyongyang to the Hebrides, from Luther's cloister to Azusa's warehouse, the rhythm is unchanged: **confession before commission, discipline before downpour, prayer before power, humility before harvest.**

Each movement of God begins where ordinary believers dare to believe that the same Spirit who once rent the heavens still waits to be invited. The wind of the Spirit blew through different tongues, yet the sound was the same: repentance, prayer, power.

Every awakening is preceded by souls who practice the ordinary means of grace—Scripture, prayer, confession, service—until the extraordinary breaks in. Perhaps the next awakening waits not in stadiums but in secret places—among those who still believe that when the heart bends, heaven descends.

The book of *Romans* has been the spark in many such fires: Augustine in the fourth century, Luther in the sixteenth, Wesley in the eighteenth, Billy Graham in the twentieth. Each met the living Word from Paul's pen to the disciples in Rome and found the heavens torn open.

Perhaps the spark we need lies in opening that same letter again—reading and praying through the epistle where the gospel of Christ burns brighter than in any other page of Scripture.

Revival never begins with noise—it begins with *knees*.

Montana Plain: "God still rends the heavens—but mostly over bent knees. History turns when saints do."

The Preludes of Awakening — Signs in the Street

History teaches that awakening rarely comes to calm waters. Before God pours oil, He shakes foundations; before refreshment, conviction; before rejoicing, mourning.

Before every great awakening there was moral collapse, political corruption, cultural mockery of faith, youth in rebellion, and pulpits gone silent or compromised. Always, the church had grown weary of itself — and then God intervened.

Sound familiar?

We are not dying; we are being undone for mercy. America is not merely collapsing; she is being confronted. God wounds before He heals.

Our Hour — The Trumpet Sounds

Pastor, elder, saint — this is not the hour for respectability. It is the hour for repentance and readiness. God visits those who prepare Him room. We are not waiting on God; He is waiting on us. We cannot schedule revival, but we can stack the wood — He will send the fire.

In the Pulpit:
Preach sin again.
Preach Christ crucified, risen, and coming again.
Preach holiness without apology until hell trembles.
Let pulpits blaze again until darkness remembers it has limits.

In the Church:
Restore prayer meetings and family worship.

Restore confession, reconciliation, and reverence.

In the Home:
Fathers, bless your households.
Mothers, teach the word of God.
Children, pray bold prayers.
Turn off the noise; turn on worship.

In the Heart:
Repent proudly. Forgive quickly. Fast secretly. Seek God earnestly. Worship joyously.

Field Guide for the Remnant

Do not ask, *Will America repent?* Ask, *Will I? Will we?* God saves nations one altar at a time.
Prepare the Ground: humble yourself, turn from sin, unclutter your soul.
Plant the Seed: gather two or three, pray and do not stop, break bread, confess, seek His face.
Expect the Rain: for God will come — not because we deserve it, but because He loves mercy and remembers dust.

Montana Plain: "Faith's muscles grow where comfort quits."

A Watchman's Prayer

Lord of awakening, rend the heavens and come down. Shake what must be shaken; strip what must be stripped; break what must be broken — until pride bows, sin mourns, and Your people burn with holy desire.

   Give us tears before triumph, intercession before influence, obedience before outpouring. Do it again, Lord — in this land, in this generation, in Your church, in us.

Let the tremors begin in our bones, the fire on our altars, the trumpet in our pulpits, and the awakening in our hearts.

And when You move, we will say, *Not to us, O Lord, but to Your Name be glory.*

The march is long, but the Commander does not change pace. Keep step.

The Soldier's Oath

"We are soldiers under oath to Christ."

— Tertullian (c. AD 200)

Tertullian came to Christian faith around forty years of age. Trained as a lawyer, he was accustomed to disciplined thinking, careful rhetoric, and precise writing. He spent the remainder of his life as a follower of Jesus—never a priest—trying to understand his faith and explain it to others. In *De Baptismo*, the first book ever written on Christian baptism, he sought words strong enough to capture what it meant to belong to Christ.

In the Roman world, soldiers swore an oath—the *sacramentum*—to the emperor. It was not symbolic. It was a binding vow of allegiance, taken publicly and carried unto death if required. Once sworn, the soldier no longer belonged to himself. His life, his obedience, and his future were placed under the command of the emperor of the Roman Empire.

When Tertullian searched for language to describe Christian baptism, he reached for that oath. Baptism, he said, is our *sacramentum*—our pledge of loyalty to Christ. Not a private sentiment. Not a rite of passage. An oath of allegiance to a new Lord.

To be baptized into Christ is to enlist under His banner. We move at His command. We stand where He places us. We do not choose the battlefield—only our faithfulness upon it.

The armor of God is not reserved for a clerical class or a spiritual elite; it is issued to every believer who has sworn the oath. From the moment we pass through the waters, we are no longer civilians. We belong to the King, and we take our place in the line—not as volunteers when convenient, but as soldiers of the Kingdom of God bound by love, obedience, and unshakable loyalty, even unto death.

12

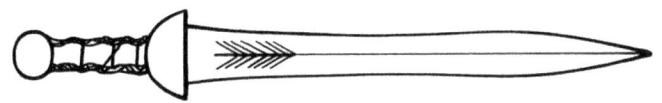

The Commissioning: When the Church Stands

"Therefore take up the whole armor of God, that you may be able to withstand in the evil day, and having done all, to stand." — Ephesians 6:13

There comes a moment in every campaign when the orders are repeated—not because the soldiers have forgotten them, but because the hour demands fresh resolve. This is that moment.

The church has studied her enemy, fortified her lines, and tended her wounded. Now comes the call not merely to believe, but to stand.

This is the recommissioning—the renewal of our vows to the Commander who has never surrendered a single inch of truth.

Before the trumpet can sound across the ranks, the commanders must awaken. Before the soldiers can march, the church must remember her calling. Before the world can see light, the people of God must rise from sleep.

This is not a new message—it is the original commission, ringing again through the centuries: *Be watchful. Stand firm. Act like men. Be strong.*

The Awakening of the Commanders
Every army rises or falls by the wakefulness of its commanders. Before troops can march, captains must see the field clearly, hear the trumpet distinctly, and lead without apology.

For too long, too many pastors have mistaken the call to shepherd for an invitation to settle. They have become chaplains to comfort rather than captains of conviction.

The flock does not need a lullaby; it needs a call to arms. The culture does not tremble when the church whispers—it trembles when the pulpit thunders.

Reclaim the Pulpit as the Armory
The sermon was never meant to be a speech; it is a briefing before battle. In the pulpit, weapons are issued, strategies clarified, morale renewed. The word of God is not a decoration for the sanctuary—it is the arsenal of heaven. When a preacher opens the Bible and says, "*Thus saith the Lord*," he is not offering an opinion but delivering orders from the High Command.

Every truth proclaimed is a sword unsheathed; every error corrected, a shield raised; every promise declared, a banner lifted over the field.

When pulpits lose that sense of holy gravity, the church becomes a lecture hall instead of a barracks. But when a preacher stands as herald rather than host—when he trembles before God more than he fears man—the congregation rises with courage.

Montana Plain: "If God's word is our sword, the pulpit is our forge—and you don't sharpen steel with velvet."

Recover the Call to Equip

Paul's charge still rings across the centuries: God gave leaders *"to equip the saints for the work of ministry, for building up the body of Christ."* The word *equip*—*katartízō*—was used for mending nets and setting broken bones. It means restoring function so the body can move again. It is giving the artisan the tools necessary for the work; it is giving the warrior the armor essential for battle.

The pastor's task, then, is not to entertain spectators but to prepare soldiers. The measure of ministry is not attendance but readiness.

When the church gathers, it should feel like morning formation: soldiers reporting for duty, armor inspected, orders clarified, prayers rising like radio contact with Command. A congregation properly equipped will not scatter in fear when storms come; they will deploy in strength.

Montana Plain: "If you want a strong church, don't build a stage—build a forge. Fire tempers iron, not straw."

Resist the Temptation of the Stage

The modern age has seduced pastors with the spotlight. We have traded the prophetic mantle for a microphone. But a shepherd who fears the crowd will never lead them to green pastures.

The stage says, "Watch me." The pulpit says, "Follow Him." The stage seeks applause; the pulpit seeks allegiance. Every pastor must decide which kingdom he serves—the kingdom of clicks or the Kingdom of Christ. The world does not need another influencer; it needs men and women whose lives influence eternity.

Montana Plain: "If the pulpit becomes a stage, the cross becomes a prop."

A Charge to the Shepherds

Shepherds of the flock, hear the word of the Lord: lay down the mantle of celebrity and take up the mantle of courage. Feed the sheep, but warn the wolves. Preach grace, but tell the truth about sin. Equip the saints, but examine your own heart first. Lead not from comfort, but from conviction. You were not called to survive this age—you were called to stand in it.

When Paul faced the executioner, he said, *"I have fought the good fight."* That was not the boast of a man who built empires; it was the testimony of a man who stayed faithful.

If the trumpet gives a clear sound, the soldiers will know which way to march. If the pulpit speaks with courage, the people will learn to stand.

"When the leaders awaken, the ranks begin to move."

The Mobilization of the Ranks

"The people who know their God shall be strong and carry out great exploits." — Daniel 11:32

An army is only as strong as its soldiers. The church was never meant to be a gallery of spectators watching their leaders fight; she is a living army—every believer armed, trained, and deployed. From the beginning, God has always moved through ordinary people with extraordinary obedience.

When pulpits fall silent, pews can still sing. When leaders falter, the Spirit recruits the willing.

The world calls them laymen. Heaven calls them soldiers.

Reframe the Identity

In the vocabulary of the Kingdom there is no divide between clergy and laity—only the *laos*, the people of God. Every believer is a priest, a servant, and a warrior in Christ's army. The Holy Spirit is not reserved for an elite few; He is the issuing officer of every saint's commission.

Peter's banner still flies over the church: *"You are a chosen generation, a royal priesthood, a holy nation, a people for God's own possession."* Titles confer nothing; the Spirit gives everything.

You do not need a platform to wield authority—you need truth in your heart and obedience in your hands. The armor of God is not ornamental; it is standard issue for every soul that confesses Christ. The moment you believe, you are enlisted.

Montana Plain: "There's no back row in God's army. If you can breathe and pray, you're in the fight."

Obedience over Position: The Pattern that Never Changes

When God shakes a nation, He rarely starts with the powerful. He looks for the willing.

- Gideon was hiding when God called him to victory.
- Deborah judged Israel with courage beneath a palm tree.
- Philip, one of the seven, preached Christ in Samaria when persecution scattered the saints.
- Tertullian, unordained and unassuming, wrote words that outlived empires.
- Jeremiah Lanphier, a New York businessman, simply opened his doors for prayer in 1857—and a revival swept the land.

The pattern never changes: God ignites the willing, not the well-placed. When pulpits fall silent, pews begin to prophesy. When institutions decay, the Spirit stirs individuals.

Obedience beats position every time.

Montana Plain: "If you're waiting for a title before you serve, you'll still be waiting when the war's over."

Renew the Vision

The church is not a refuge for spectators; she is a rally point for soldiers. The Holy Spirit does not promote—He deploys. Every believer is sent, armed, and assigned a sector of the field.

Your workplace is your mission ground.

Your home is your training camp.

Your community is your patrol area.

When the church gathers, she regroups; when she scatters, she advances. The early believers understood this rhythm. They prayed in homes, sang in prisons, preached in markets, and died in arenas—and the world changed. Somewhere along the way, the church traded her armor for attendance sheets. We must recover the call to go again—not as tourists, but as troops.

Montana Plain: "Sunday's for regrouping; Monday's for marching."

A Rallying Cry for the People of God

You have been equipped with more than information—you have been entrusted with revelation. You carry the same Spirit that raised Jesus from the dead, wear the same armor Paul described in Ephesians 6, and follow the same Commander who conquered death.

This is not a battle for survival but for souls. The time is not someday—it is now. Take up your shield of faith. Sharpen your sword of the Spirit. Fasten your belt of truth. Stand in the armor of light.

You are not the reserve corps waiting for orders—you are the front line of the Kingdom. When you walk into the world filled with the Spirit, hell loses ground. When you pray, speak truth, and live righteously, you are already advancing the cause of Christ.

Montana Plain: "If you've got breath in your lungs and truth in your heart, you're on active duty."

The Church: Field Hospital, Fortress, and Forward Operating Base

"I will build My church, and the gates of hell shall not prevail against it." — Matthew 16:18

The church is not a monument to what God once did; she is a living organism through whom He still moves. She is a body, a bride, and an army. And in this confused and fragmenting age, she must again become all three at once.

We have too often treated her as a shelter when she was meant to be a stronghold, as a retreat when she was meant to be a rally point. Yet the true church is both compassionate and courageous: a Field Hospital, a Fortress, and a Forward Operating Base for the Kingdom of God.

The Field Hospital — Healing on the Front Lines

The first duty of the church is mercy. We live in a world riddled with shrapnel—wounds from sin, betrayal, despair, and confusion—and the wounded do not need condemnation before they can be healed. When she is true to her Lord, the church binds the brokenhearted and lifts the fallen. Like the Good Samaritan, she pours oil and wine on the wounds: oil for soothing, wine for cleansing—grace and truth together.

The pew becomes a triage station, the altar a place of surgery, the fellowship hall a recovery ward. No wound is too deep for Christ's healing, no sinner too far for His mercy. But mercy was never meant to end in comfort; it was meant to lead to commission. The healed are rearmed. The forgiven are redeployed. Every testimony is a soldier returned to the fight.

Montana Plain: "You don't patch a soldier just to send him home—you patch him to send him back to the line."

The Fortress — Guarding the Truth
Every army needs strongholds—places where the line holds, where the standard flies high, and where the weary can rest under protection. The church must once again become such a place—not a castle of pride, but a bastion of truth. Inside her walls, the word of God is preserved; here the doctrines of the faith are not optional opinions but the lifeblood of endurance. Within her gates, heresy finds resistance, not applause.

The fortress does not exist to hide the faithful from the world; it exists to keep the world from hollowing out the faith. In its courts, saints are refined and trained; from its gates, truth marches out again.

Montana Plain: "A real fortress doesn't just keep things out—it keeps the fire in."

The Forward Operating Base — The Church on the Move
Here we reach the mission center of the Kingdom. The church was never designed to be static; she is a moving column, a living outpost of heaven in hostile territory. Every Sunday the assembly regroups, re-equips, and receives new orders. Every benediction

is a deployment. Every amen is the sound of boots stepping toward the field.

Jesus said the gates of hell would not prevail—and gates, remember, are defensive. It is hell that holds the high walls now, and the church, armed with truth and love, is the besieging force. The gates of deception cannot withstand the truth of the Gospel. The gates of despair cannot withstand the light of hope. The gates of death cannot withstand the power of resurrection.

When believers step out of the sanctuary with conviction and compassion, the front lines move forward. Every conversation becomes a skirmish for the soul; every act of faith becomes an advance of the Kingdom.

Montana Plain: "We don't just gather for church—we gather as the church, then we deploy."

The Recommissioning

Every generation faces its own Goliath. Some see him in government, others in culture, still others in the corrosion of conscience. But the true battleground has never changed—it lies within the human heart.

Paul wrote his charge to the Ephesians not to stir rebellion but to inspire readiness. He knew that the fiercest wars are not fought with steel or stone, but with truth, righteousness, faith, salvation, and the word of God. These are not accessories for Sunday—they are essential for survival every day.

To stand in this hour demands more than sentiment; it requires spiritual formation, disciplined devotion, and holy defiance.

Montana Plain: "Faith without formation is like a rifle without rounds—it looks good 'til you need it."

The Orders from Command

"Put on the whole armor of God." That phrase is not suggestion but imperative—not optional equipment for the zealous few, but the uniform of every believer.

- The Belt of Truth fastens first, because everything else hangs from it.
- The Breastplate of Righteousness guards the heart from compromise.
- The Shoes of Readiness carry peace, not panic, into the fray.
- The Shield of Faith quenches the fiery darts of doubt and deception.
- The Helmet of Salvation protects the mind with assurance and identity.
- And the Sword of the Spirit cuts through lies with the word of God itself.

This armor is not ornamental—it is operational. It must be donned, checked, and worn into the field daily.

Montana Plain: "You can't win Monday's fight with Sunday's sermon—you've got to wear your gear every day."

The Marching Orders

A soldier does not choose the battlefield; the Commander does. We do not fight for victory—we fight from it. The cross settled the outcome; our task is to live out that triumph.

Wherever truth is mocked, stand.
Wherever faith is tested, stand.
Wherever Christ's name is silenced, speak—and stand again.

This war will not be won by outrage but by obedience; not by anger but by endurance; not by politics but by presence. If revival comes, it will not begin in Washington or Rome, but in living rooms and prayer closets. The greatest awakenings always begin when ordinary believers act like soldiers again.

Montana Plain: "The revolution of righteousness starts one kneeling heart at a time."

The Unity of the Ranks

The enemy has long known that a divided church is a defeated church. He fears not our programs or platforms—he fears our unity under Christ. So the order goes out: ***close ranks***.

Stand shoulder to shoulder.

No rivalry, no jealousy, no civilian entanglements.

If one falters, another lifts him up.

If one falls, another takes his place.

If one prays, a hundred stand stronger.

The line must hold—not because of who we are, but because of Whose we are.

Montana Plain: "If we ever learn to march together, hell's got a problem."

The Final Charge

This is not the hour for retreat. It is the hour for recommissioning. The same Spirit who hovered over the chaos now inhabits the hearts of those willing to stand. The same power that rolled away the stone now calls us to roll back the darkness.

So stand when you pray.

Stand when you preach.

Stand when the world mocks and the winds howl.

For when the church stands—healed, fortified, and advancing—
the gates of hell cannot hold.

The Soldier's Prayer
"Not by might, nor by power, but by My Spirit," says the Lord of hosts. — Zechariah 4:6

Commander of Heaven's Armies,
we stand before You—
weary, yet willing; small in the eyes of the world, yet chosen in Yours.
We do not ask for ease; we ask for endurance.
We do not seek escape; we seek empowerment.

Fill us, O Holy Spirit.
Breathe into these dry bones until they stand again—clothed with courage, quickened with love, and armed with truth.
We have seen enough of our strength to know it will not do.
We have trusted our wit and our weapons and found them wanting.
So now we surrender the reins—heart, mind, will, and way—into Your command.

Forgive our pride that mistook strategy for spirituality,
our comfort that dulled conviction,
our fear that kept us silent when truth was on trial.
Cleanse us from the cowardice that bows to culture
and the apathy that calls it peace.
Spirit of the Living God, fall fresh upon us.
Renew the minds of pastors who have grown tired of the fight.
Reignite the hearts of believers who have forgotten their first love.

Let the pulpits burn again with righteousness,
and the pews tremble again with repentance.
Raise up Gideons in hiding,
Deborahs with discernment,
Philips who run toward the chariots,
and faithful saints who hold the line when others fall away.
Teach our hands to war in prayer,
our lips to speak with grace and truth,
our feet to carry the Gospel of peace.
Make our homes outposts of light in the gathering dark.
Let our unity be our shield,
our love our banner,
and our holiness our strength.

May Your power be displayed not through our dominion,
but through our devotion—
that even our enemies may see and say, "God is among them."
When the world rages, steady us.
When fear whispers, still us.
When the call comes, send us.
Until that day when the battle is over and the trumpet sounds,
keep us faithful
at our post—
watchmen on the wall, warriors in the Word, servants of the King.

And when You count the faithful, Lord, let it be said of us:
They stood.

In the mighty name of Jesus Christ,
the Captain of our Salvation—
Amen.

*"Behold, your king is coming to you;
righteous and having salvation,
humble and mounted on a donkey."*

— Zechariah 9:9

13

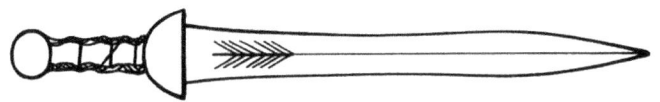

Warrior-King

He was never naïve. That is the first thing the Gospels make clear about Jesus. From the opening months of His ministry to the final week in Jerusalem, He walked with a clarity of mind and a clear discernment that embarrassed His enemies and exposed their motives. Spiritual warfare was not an abstraction to Him; it pressed into His days through political traps, religious conspiracies, and the relentless scrutiny of those (mostly of the religious sects) who wanted Him gone.

Mark 3 offers the first revealing glimpse of the collusions Jesus faced throughout His ministry. Jesus entered the synagogue knowing exactly who was waiting for Him. The Pharisees had not come to worship—they had come as observers, watching Him "*so that they might accuse Him.*"

The man with the withered hand stood before Him, and with all eyes fixed, Jesus healed him. The text says He was angered—grieved by the hardness of their hearts. And in that moment of compassion for the man, the first political-religious alliance formed against Him.

The Pharisees team up with the Herodians—**a political-religious alliance** that would be shocking to any Jewish observer.
The Pharisees hated Rome.

The Herodians loved Rome.
But they hated Jesus more.

This is the first recorded assassination plot against Him. Jesus' ministry was barely underway and the power blocs of Israel already wanted Him dead. Mark records the result without ornament: ***"The Pharisees went out and immediately began conspiring with the Herodians against Him, as to how they might kill Him."***

This was early—very early—in His public work. And Jesus knew it. He understood the nature of the opposition, the shape of their power, and the stakes of their plotting. His discernment never dulled.

Years later, in the final week of His life, the same coalition reappeared—still aligned, still hunting. This time their trap was crafted around the tribute tax (Matthew 22:15-22). The question—*"Is it lawful to pay the tax to Caesar or not?"*—was not a theological inquiry. It was a weapon, a trap.

A "yes" answer would label Jesus a compromiser of Israel's allegiance to the one true God. A "no" answer would classify Him as a revolutionary, guilty of sedition against Rome. It was a political minefield with no safe passage. But Jesus did not step into the trap. He exposed it to the frustration of His enemies.

"Bring me the tribute coin," He said. Notice that he did not call for just any coin; He asked for a *tribute* coin. And in the sacred precincts of the Temple—where such a coin was forbidden—one of His adversaries produced it. They themselves (probably one of the Herodians) were holding the idolatrous currency they pretended to despise. Jesus lifted it, held it in the light, and asked the only question that mattered: ***"Whose image is this?"***

Not whose picture. But whose *image—imago*, the mark of ownership, allegiance, and worship. Caesar's face was stamped on the coin. But God's image—*imago Dei*—was stamped on the human being.

"Render to Caesar what is Caesar's," He said, **"and to God what is God's**."

It was not merely a brilliant answer—it was a devastating one. Jesus avoided the political snare, exposed their hypocrisy, upheld God's sovereignty, and walked away unscathed.

These two incidents bookend the ministry of Jesus —
• the synagogue showdown (Mark 3) at the beginning,
• the tribute-coin trap (Matthew 22) at the end —
and between them stands a Messiah who walked the battlefield with absolute clarity, *never once confusing the war He came to fight with the weapons His enemies used against Him.*

He did not fight with a sword. He fought with truth.

And that is the pattern: Jesus recognized His enemies; He exposed their schemes; He walked straight into hostile spaces—but He never raised a weapon. He practiced the very ethic He taught His disciples: ***be wise as serpents, and harmless as doves.***

This is crucial for the moment this book addresses. We face ideological enemies, cultural enemies, and political enemies—but the Christian does not fight with blades or bullets. Our war is spiritual, intellectual, moral. The weapons of our warfare, Paul reminds us, "*are not carnal*," yet they are powerful enough to "*pull down strongholds*," the entrenched systems of thought and deception that rule minds and cultures.

Jesus Himself modeled what it means to resist evil without

mirroring its methods. He was neither blind nor passive. He confronted corruption directly. He exposed manipulation without being manipulated. He understood the political complexities of His age—Roman taxation, Herodian collaboration, Pharisaic legalism, Temple economics—and He navigated that terrain with unswerving obedience to His Father and absolute clarity about the true battlefield.

That same pattern appears in our own time in the life of the man whose death opens these companion books. Charlie Kirk walked onto America's college campuses knowing full well the ideological hostility he would face. He understood the terrain—Gramscian cultural theory embedded in classrooms, Frankfurt School critique shaping curriculum, activist bureaucracies policing speech, and a generation being formed in assumptions hostile to faith, family, and freedom. He recognized the opposition, anticipated the traps, and prepared for the battles he would face—yet he fought them with the same non-kinetic weapons Jesus used: truth, courage, clarity, and unflinching moral conviction.

Charlie did not arm young people with violence; he armed them with worldview.

    He did not stir aggression; he stirred discernment.

    He did not teach rebellion; he taught responsibility
        and reason.

    He faced enemies, but he did not become one.

    In this, Charlie followed the battle plan of Jesus to the letter. He fought in the realm where the true war is waged—ideas, conscience, language, persuasion, truth—and it is for that very reason that the enemies of liberty hated him.

    To follow Jesus is not to withdraw from conflict but to recognize the real arena in which conflict must be waged. Jesus knew who plotted His death, but He never called His disciples to arms. He knew the political traps set before Him, but He never answered them on their terms. He understood the spiritual forces animating the visible opposition, and He addressed the battle at its root—not its symptoms.

And this becomes the lesson for believers today:

We do not deny the presence of enemies.
We deny them the terms of the battle.

Spiritual warfare requires clarity, courage, and discernment.
Enemies exist.
Plots exist.
Ideologies exist.
Hostilities exist.

Our weapons are spiritual: truth, righteousness, faith, the gospel of peace, the salvation of God, Scripture, and prayer. The Christian warrior stands as Jesus stood—discerning, unafraid, uncompromising, and entirely committed to God's kingdom rather than earthly retaliation.

Jesus won His battles without ever lifting a sword.
Charlie fought his battles the same way.
And the church must do likewise today.

When the warriors of God engage in battle, the church is revived and the nation awakened.

Unhinderedly

The last word of the book of Acts in the Greek text from the hand of Luke, the physician, is *akōlytōs*—unhinderedly. Luke was declaring that the gospel had overcome every barrier and continued to spread without restraint. If that is to remain true in our republic, the army of God must arise and take its place along the battle line drawn by the enemies of the gospel of Christ.

> ***"The most important thing is to bring people to Christ. The second most important thing is to preserve the freedom to do the most important thing."***
> *— William J. Federer*

Every enemy named in the pages of the companion volumes, *The Battle for the Republic* and *Called to Stand*, understands this truth, even when the church forgets it. Tyranny—whether dressed in Marxist theory, religious absolutism, or technocratic control—does not merely oppose Christian ideas; it seeks to silence Christian witness. Where such powers prevail, the Gospel is restricted, the church is surveilled, and believers are pressured, imprisoned, or killed for refusing to bow.

These are not hypothetical dangers. They are historical facts—and present realities across much of the world. The question before us is not whether conflict exists, but whether we will stand while there is still ground to hold. The armor of God is not issued for parade duty. It is given so the church may remain faithful, fearless, and free to proclaim Christ until the trumpet sounds again.

Epilogue

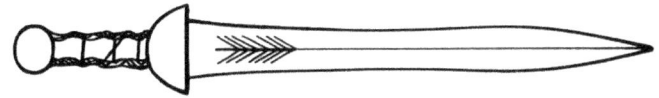

The Trumpet at Dawn
A Soldier's Oath—a Benediction for Those Who Stand

"Having done all… stand." — Ephesians 6:13

When the church of any generation reaches a crossroads, God does not first raise up princes or politicians. He awakens ordinary saints with extraordinary conviction. They are not escapists seeking shelter; they are believers who refuse to yield to the darkness.

This is our hour.
The shaking has come.
The lines are drawn.
The hosts of heaven lean over the rails.

And the command is not retreat — but *stand.*
Stand clothed in Christ.
Stand rooted in truth.
Stand beneath the banner of the Lamb.
Stand until the dawn breaks and the trumpet sounds again.

For we do not war as the world wars. We do not strap steel plates or sharpen earthly blades. Our weapons are older, stronger, eternal — **truth, righteousness, the gospel of peace, faith, salvation, the word of God, persevering prayer.**

We do not stand unarmed.
We do not stand afraid.
And we do not stand alone.

The Armor Declaration of the Remnant
This is no metaphor. It is survival. It is commissioning. It is covenant.

This day, O Lord, I stand and I suit up.

The Helmet of Salvation — guard my mind; break the lies with truth; silence accusation; steady my identity. I am bought, sealed, secured, and sent.

The Breastplate of Righteousness — not my merit, but Your mercy. Guard my affections and purify my motives. Let no shame, pride, or bitterness take root in me.

The Belt of Truth — fasten me to Your word, not to culture, mood, or shifting opinion. Truth holds me together; You hold me together.

The Gospel Shoes of Peace — guide my steps. Make me stable in trouble, gentle among souls, bold in witness. Wherever I walk, heaven walks.

The Shield of Faith — I lift it high. Let every dart of doubt, accusation, or fear be quenched. My faith is not in outcomes, but in the Unchanging One.

The Sword of the Spirit — place Your word on my tongue. Let "*It is written*" be my war cry. Give me a sharp mind for truth and a soft heart for souls.

And above all, **praying always** — alert, watchful, yielded. Armor is not for sitting; it is for standing and advancing.

I am covered. I am called. I am kept. I am commissioned.
Not in fear, but in faith.
Not for comfort, but for combat in a holy war already won.

The enemy may come in like a flood, but the Lord — the Man of War, the Lamb who reigns, the Lion of Judah whose eyes burn like fire — He raises the standard.

So I say again:
I am a warrior.
I am a watchman.
I am a pilgrim under orders.
I am fully awake, fully armed.
I will stand.
In Jesus' name. Amen.

A Final Word to the Faithful

When you close this book, the real battle begins.
Not in Washington.
Not in boardrooms.
Not on screens.

It begins in pulpits and prayer closets, in living rooms and human hearts.

The world does not fear a church that sings — it fears a church that *stands*.

So drink deeply, saint.
Fast often.
Weep sometimes.
Preach the word.
Raise the banner.
Pray without ceasing.

And when your strength fails — and it will — stand anyway.
For the Captain of our salvation stands with you.

"Be strong in the Lord and in the power of His might." — Ephesians 6:10

The trumpet has sounded.
The armor is fitted.
The hour is late.
The King is near.

Having done all — stand.

Appendix

Church Readiness Assessment

Here's a **Church Readiness Assessment**. It's practical, evaluative, and invitational—something that could as a study guide for pastors and church leaders to help their churches.

This **Readiness Assessment** may prove to be one of the most practical pieces in *Called to Stand.* It takes the prophetic message of the book — the call to courage, repentance, and formation — and hands you a tool for action. It's the bridge between conviction and obedience.

It is a mirror and a map:

- **A mirror** showing pastors and believers where drift has already occurred.

- **A map** showing where to rebuild, beginning with Word, Spirit, and daily discipline.

Introduction to the Church Readiness Assessment

"Examine Yourselves, Whether You Be in the Faith." — 2 Corinthians 13:5

The *Church Readiness Assessment* is not a scorecard. It isn't meant to measure success, but to reveal drift — the quiet kind that happens when good people get comfortable in a fallen age. It's an invitation to honesty before God, to ask the questions most churches avoid until the damage is done. It is also a map showing where to rebuild, beginning with Word, Spirit, and daily discipline.

Throughout *Called to Stand,* we have traced how truth was eroded, how courage waned, and how the church's voice softened under cultural pressure. Yet the problem is not beyond repair. Scripture tells us that judgment begins at the house of God — but so does revival. Renewal always begins with awareness, confession, and repentance.

This tool offers a way to begin that work.

It follows three dimensions of learning — what we **know** (cognitive), what we **love** (affective), and what we **practice** (behavioral). Together, they form a simple framework for pastors, leaders, and believers to evaluate whether their ministries and lives are aligned with the mission of Christ or have drifted toward the values of the world.

Use it prayerfully. Don't rush it. Sit with each question. Discuss it with your leadership, your small group, or your own heart before God. If you find weakness, give thanks — for that's where the Spirit begins His work of strength.

This is not about perfection; it's about direction. The aim is not to condemn, but to **rekindle** — to call the church back to her first love, her true message, and her holy mission.

"Nevertheless I have this against you, that you have left your first love. Remember therefore from where you have fallen; repent, and do the works you did at first." — Revelation 2:4–5

Let this assessment be a holy pause — a moment of clarity in a noisy age. The question is not whether the culture is dark, but whether the lampstand still burns bright.

May the Spirit who convicts also comfort, the truth that wounds also heal, and the Church of Jesus Christ stand again in the power of His might.

The Church Readiness Assessment: A Mirror and a Map

Evaluating the Church's Readiness to Stand in an Age of Collapse

"If the trumpet gives an uncertain sound, who shall prepare himself to the battle?" — 1 Corinthians 14:8

This assessment was designed to help pastors, elders, and believers translate the message of this book into measurable renewal.

The Church Readiness Assessment is not a scorecard; it's a mirror. It isn't meant to measure success, but to reveal drift—the quiet kind that happens when good people grow comfortable in a fallen age. It's an invitation to honesty before God, a chance to ask the questions most churches avoid until the damage is done. It's also a map showing where to rebuild—beginning again with Word, Spirit, and daily discipline.

Before a church can take the field, it must first examine its ranks. This assessment helps pastors, leaders, and members measure whether they have been quietly captured by the spirit of the age or are standing firm in the truth. It follows the three classic domains of learning—**cognitive**, **affective**, and **behavioral (psychomotor)**—and applies them to the life of the church.

I. **The Cognitive Domain — Truth and Teaching**

II. **The Affective Domain — Values and Loyalties**

III. **The Behavioral Domain — Practice and Engagement**

IV. **Interpreting the Results — From Drift to Deployment**

V. **From Assessment to Action — Steps Toward Renewal**

Each section includes reflection questions and a 1–5 rating scale:
1 – Absent   2 – Weak   3 – Emerging   4 – Strong   5 – Evident and Reproducing

I. Cognitive Domain — Truth and Teaching

What we believe and proclaim

The pulpit is the helm of the church; when it drifts, the whole ship turns off course.

When pulpits lose their voice, culture fills the silence. The cognitive domain measures whether truth still governs our preaching, teaching, and public witness.

Questions for Reflection

How many sermons or lessons this year have been drawn directly from Scripture, verse by verse, compared to topical or therapeutic messages?

Are doctrines such as creation, sin, redemption, judgment, and the Kingdom of God clearly taught, or assumed and rarely explained?

When cultural controversies arise, are they addressed biblically or avoided for fear of offense?

Does the language of your church's teaching echo Scripture ("sin," "repentance," "holiness") or the language of secular culture ("inclusion," "affirmation," "personal truth")?

Are members being trained to read and interpret the Bible for themselves?

Indicators of Drift

Biblical illiteracy among members

Sermons measured by tone rather than truth

A shrinking vocabulary of holiness and repentance

Score (1–5): _____

II. Affective Domain — Values and Loyalties

What we love, honor, and fear

A church's heart is revealed in its calendar and its checkbook. What does your church celebrate most? That question will tell you what it worships.

The affective domain measures alignment of our emotions and priorities with the heart of God.

Questions for Reflection

What proportion of your church's budget and energy goes toward evangelism, discipleship, and missions compared to marketing, technology, or entertainment?

What issues stir the greatest passion among your people—revival and repentance, or politics and personalities?

Are members more concerned about cultural approval than divine approval?

When culture celebrates what God forbids, does the church remain silent to avoid controversy?

Does your fellowship demonstrate compassion without compromising conviction?

Indicators of Drift

- Fear of man outweighing fear of God
- Applause-seeking, peacekeeping leadership
- Emotional resonance with worldly causes more than gospel mandates

Score (1–5): _____

III. Behavioral Domain — Practice and Engagement

What we actually do

Belief and love must take form in obedience. The behavioral domain measures whether conviction produces visible action.

Questions for Reflection

Are members personally sharing their faith and engaging their communities with the gospel?

Are pastors and leaders modeling courage in public and private life?

Does the church speak to moral and civic responsibility—encouraging believers to vote, serve, and stand as salt and light?

Do worship, prayer, and study gatherings equip people for mission, or merely provide comfort?

How many disciples have been personally mentored and released to serve in the last year?

Indicators of Drift

High activity with little transformation—much motion, little movement.

Comfort prioritized over courage

Discipleship replaced by programming

Score (1–5): _____

IV. Interpreting the Results— From Drift to Deployment

Domain	1–2	3	4–5
Cognitive	Truth Drift	Truth Recovery	Truth Declared
Affective	Heart Drift	Heart Awakening	Heart Aligned
Behavioral	Mission Drift	Mission Renewal	Mission Deployed

Composite Score: Add the three domain scores and divide by 3.

- **4.0–5.0 – Combat-Ready Church:** truth-anchored, Spirit-empowered, actively discipling and deploying.

- **3.0–3.9 – Recovering Church:** awareness has begun; course correction needed; revival is possible.

- **1.0–2.9 – Captured Church:** cultural captivity evident; repentance and re-formation urgent.

V. From Assessment to Action — Steps Toward Renewal

Repent where drift is revealed. Every revival begins with confession.

Rebuild the foundations. Return Scripture to the center of preaching and prayer to the center of power.

Retrain the ranks. Equip believers through personal disciplines and biblical discipleship.

Re-engage the field. Deploy members into their communities as witnesses, servants, and citizens of the Kingdom.

The goal is not perfection but progression — movement toward faithfulness in every domain.

"Be watchful, stand firm in the faith, act like men, be strong. Let all that you do be done in love." — 1 Corinthians 16:13–14

Reflection for the Road:
The test is not whether our programs succeed, but whether our people stand. When the battle is joined, the faithful will already be formed. Revival begins long before the trumpet sounds — it begins in the hearts that are ready to stand.

Gifted by Grace

God has empowered every believer in Jesus Christ with the Presence of the Holy Spirit. The disciples were told to remain in Jerusalem, to not attempt ministry on their own. They were to wait for the empowerment of the Spirit of God.

On the Day of Pentecost, the Spirit came with power accompanied by phenomena—the sound of a rushing mighty wind, tongues of fire sat upon each follower of Jesus gathered in that upper room in prayer. And in that moment He baptized them and formed them into the church, the Body of Christ upon the earth.

These filled and empowered believers then went into the crowd speaking the gospel to the multitude that had gathered from the nations of the earth to celebrate the feast of Pentecost. Thousands heard and professed faith in Christ that day. The battles of the Kingdom are not fought by professionals but by the prepared.

Every believer is equipped by the Spirit with gifts necessary for the strengthening of the church and the advancement of the gospel. These are not optional capacities; they are your weapons in a world at war. The tools in the following appendix are not included merely for reflection, but for deployment. Discover your gifts, develop them, and then direct them — for the fight needs every soldier.

Paul on gifts of grace

***1** Now concerning spiritual gifts, brethren, I would not have you ignorant. **2** Ye know that ye were Gentiles, carried away unto these dumb idols, even as ye were led. **3** Wherefore I give you to understand, that no man speaking by the Spirit of God calleth Jesus accursed: and that no man can say that Jesus is the Lord, but by the Holy Ghost.*

***4** Now there are diversities of gifts, but the same Spirit.*

***5** And there are differences of administrations, but the same Lord.*

***6** And there are diversities of operations, but it is the same God which worketh all in all. **7** But the manifestation of the Spirit is given to every man to profit withal.*

***8** For to one is given by the Spirit the word of wisdom; to another the word of knowledge by the same Spirit; **9** To another faith by the same Spirit; to another the gifts of healing by the same Spirit; **10** To another the working of miracles; to another prophecy; to another discerning of spirits; to another divers kinds of tongues; to another the interpretation of tongues:*

***11** But all these worketh that one and the selfsame Spirit, dividing to every man severally as he will. **12** But as the body is one, and hath many members, and all the members of that body, being many, are one body: so also is Christ.*

***13** For by one Spirit are we all baptized into one body, whether we be Jews or Gentiles, whether we be bond or free; and have been all made to drink into one Spirit.*

—1 Corinthians 12:1-13

The Spiritual Gifts Inventory

Directions: Take the inventory at this time. The *Spiritual Gifts Inventory*[1] will aid you in discovering and understanding your spiritual gifts. Your honest thoughtful response to the inventory will help in obtaining the best results. You will be given instructions for scoring and interpreting the inventory later.

Your response choices are:
5 - Highly characteristic

4 - Most of the time

3 - Frequently

2 - Occasionally

1 - Not at all

Before you begin—just a few comments...
This is not a test, so ***there are no wrong answers***. The inventory consists of 103 items. Some of these reflect concrete actions; others are descriptive traits; and still others are statements of belief. You are asked to indicate how descriptive the item is of you.

Record your response by placing in the blank beside each item the number which corresponds to the answer you want.

Do not spend too much time on any one item. Remember, it's not a test. Mark the extent to which you feel the item is descriptive of you. Usually your immediate response is best.

Please give a response for *each item*. Do not skip any items. And be willing to indicate that an item is highly descriptive or not of you. For instance, if you give a "safe" 3 to each answer, you will be less likely to identify the grace gifts or gifts God has given you to equip you for your particular ministry.

Work at your own pace.

Spiritual Gifts Inventory

_____ 1. I have the ability to organize ideas, resources, time, and people effectively.

_____ 2. I am willing to study and prepare for the task of teaching.

_____ 3. I am able to relate the truths of God to specific situations.

_____ 4. I inspire persons to right actions by pointing out the blessings of this path.

_____ 5. I have a God-given ability to help others grow in their faith.

_____ 6. I possess a special ability to communicate the truth of salvation.

_____ 7. I am sensitive to the hurts of people.

_____ 8. I experience joy in meeting needs through sharing possessions.

_____ 9. I enjoy study.

_____ 10. I have delivered God's messages of warning and judgment.

_____ 11. I am able to sense the true motivations of persons and movements.

_____ 12. I trust God in difficult situations.

_____ 13. I have a strong desire to contribute to the establishment of new churches.

_____ 14. I feel God has used me in a supernatural event.

____ 15. I enjoy doing things for people in need.

____ 16. I am aware of a special appropriation of God's healing power through myself.

____ 17. I have been moved to express such intense spiritual feelings that what came from my mouth was unintelligible to most people.

____ 18. Words or thoughts come to me in an inspiring way after a message in an unknown language is delivered in group worship.

____ 19. I can delegate and assign meaningful work.

____ 20. I have an ability and desire to teach.

____ 21. I am usually able to analyze a situation correctly.

____ 22. I have a tendency to encourage and reward others.

____ 23. I am willing to take the initiative in helping other Christians grow in their faith.

____ 24. I am unafraid to share with lost people.

____ 25. I have an acute awareness of such emotions as loneliness, pain, fear, and anger in others.

____ 26. I am a cheerful giver.

____ 27. I spend time digging into facts.

____ 28. I feel that I have a message from God to deliver to others.

____ 29. I can recognize when a person is genuine/honest.

____ 30. I am willing to yield to God's will rather than question and waver.

____ 31. I would like to be more active in getting the gospel to people in other lands.

____ 32. I have been used by God to bring about supernatural changes.

____ 33. It makes me happy to do things for people in need.

____ 34. I am willing to be an instrument of healing.

____ 35. I have had an awareness of wanting to praise God in utterances which one's heart feels but which one's mind does not understand.

____ 36. I have prayed that I may interpret if someone begins speaking in tongues.

____ 37. I am successful in getting a group to do its work joyfully.

____ 38. I have the ability to plan learning approaches.

____ 39. I have been able to offer solutions to spiritual problems others are facing.

____ 40. I can identify those who need encouragement.

____ 41. I have trained Christians to be more obedient disciples of Christ.

____ 42. I am willing to do whatever it takes to see others come to Christ.

____ 43. I am attracted to people who are hurting.

_____ 44. I am a generous giver.

_____ 45. I am able to discover new truths.

_____ 46. I have spiritual insights from Scripture concerning issues and people which compel me to speak out.

_____ 47. I can sense when a person is acting in accord with God's will.

_____ 48. I can trust God even when things look dark.

_____ 49. I have a strong desire to take the gospel to places where it has never been heard.

_____ 50. I have been used by God to accomplish a miracle.

_____ 51. I enjoy helping people.

_____ 52. I understand scriptural teachings regarding healing.

_____ 53. I believe that speaking in tongues may be edifying to the Lord's Body.

_____ 54. I am able to interpret the ecstatic utterances of others.

_____ 55. I have been able to make effective and efficient plans for accomplishing the goals of a group.

_____ 56. I understand the variety of ways people learn.

_____ 57. I am often consulted when fellow Christians are struggling to make difficult decisions.

_____ 58. I think about how I can comfort and encourage others in my congregation.

_____ 59. I am able to give spiritual direction to others.

_____ 60. I am able to present the gospel to lost persons in such a way that they accept the Lord and His salvation.

_____ 61. I possess an unusual capacity to understand the feelings of those in distress.

_____ 62. I have a strong sense of stewardship based on the recognition of God's ownership of all things.

_____ 63. I know where to get information.

_____ 64. I have delivered to other persons messages which have come directly from God.

_____ 65. I can sense when a person is acting under God's leadership.

_____ 66. I try to be continually in God's will.

_____ 67. I feel I should take the gospel to people who have different beliefs from me.

_____ 68. I have been God's instrument to bring about supernatural change in lives or events.

_____ 69. I love to do things for people.

_____ 70. I am aware of the miraculous aspects of life.

_____ 71. I enjoy being with persons who speak in tongues.

_____ 72. I have prayed that I may be able to interpret tongues.

_____ 73. I am skilled in setting forth positive and precise steps of action.

_____ 74. I explain Scripture in such a way that others understand it.

____ 75. I can usually see spiritual solutions to problems.

____ 76. I am glad when people who need comfort, consolation, encouragement, and counsel seek my help.

____ 77. I am able to nurture others.

____ 78. I feel at ease in sharing Christ with nonbelievers.

____ 79. I recognize the signs of stress and distress in others.

____ 80. I desire to give generously and unpretentiously to worthwhile projects and ministries.

____ 81. I can organize facts into meaningful relationships.

____ 82. God gives me messages to deliver to His people.

____ 83. I am able to sense whether people are being honest when they tell of their religious experiences.

____ 84. I try to be available for God to use.

____ 85. I enjoy presenting the gospel to persons of other cultures and backgrounds.

____ 86. I have been used by God to bring about a powerful act which could not be explained in human terms.

____ 87. I enjoy doing little things that help people.

____ 88. I am aware of the supernatural power at work within my life.

____ 89. Speaking in tongues enables me to be more effective in all areas of my life.

____ 90. I can plan a strategy and "bring others aboard."

_____ 91. I can give a clear, uncomplicated presentation.

_____ 92. I have been able to apply biblical truth to the specific needs of my church.

_____ 93. God has used me to encourage others to live Christ-like lives.

_____ 94. I have sensed the need to help other people become more effective in their ministries.

_____ 95. I like to talk about Jesus to those who do not know Him.

_____ 96. I feel assured that a situation will change for the glory of God even when the situation seems impossible.

_____ 97. I am able to nurture others.

_____ 98. I have an awareness that God still heals people as He did in biblical times.

_____ 99. I have matured in my spiritual life as a result of speaking in tongues.

_____ 100. I sense God's intervention in events.

_____ 101. I have witnessed miraculous answers to my prayers.

_____ 102. I believe God can and does act in miraculous ways.

_____ 103. I have a burning desire to see people who are suffering be made well.

Now...score yourself.

On the following pages you will find the scoring instrument. Follow these instructions:

1. For each gift place in the boxes the number of the response you gave for each item indicated below the box.
2. For each gift add the numbers in the boxes and put the total (sum) in the "TOTAL" box.
3. For each gift divide the TOTAL by the number indicated and place the result in the "SCORE" box (round each answer to one decimal place, such as 3.7). This is your score for the gift.

[1]*Spiritual Gifts Inventory* was developed by the Baptist Sunday School Board's Adult Section of the Discipleship Training Department and is validated within a 90 percentile range of accuracy. Used by permission.

Gift   (Hint: score more quickly, fill the boxes vertically)

Leadership   ☐ + ☐ + ☐ + ☐ + ☐ +
Item 1   Item 19   Item 37   Item 55   Item 73

☐ = ☐ ÷ 6 = ☐
Item 90   TOTAL   SCORE

Teaching   ☐ + ☐ + ☐ + ☐ + ☐ +
Item 2   Item 20   Item 38   Item 56   Item 74

☐ = ☐ ÷ 6 = ☐
Item 91   TOTAL   SCORE

Knowledge   ☐ + ☐ + ☐ + ☐ + ☐ +
Item 9   Item 27   Item 45   Item 63   Item 81

☐ = ☐ ÷ 6 = ☐
Item 96   TOTAL   SCORE

Wisdom   ☐ + ☐ + ☐ + ☐ + ☐ +
Item 3   Item 21   Item 39   Item 57   Item 75

☐ = ☐ ÷ 6 = ☐
Item 92   TOTAL   SCORE

Prophecy   ☐ + ☐ + ☐ + ☐ + ☐ =
Item 4   Item 22   Item 40   Item 58   Item 76

☐ ÷ 5 = ☐
TOTAL   SCORE

Spiritual Discernment   ☐ + ☐ + ☐ + ☐ + ☐ =
Item 11   Item 29   Item 47   Item 65   Item 83

☐ ÷ 5 = ☐
TOTAL   SCORE

Encouragement   ☐ + ☐ + ☐ + ☐ + ☐ +
Item 4   Item 22   Item 40   Item 58   Item 76

☐ = ☐ ÷ 6 = ☐
Item 93   TOTAL   SCORE

Shepherding □ + □ + □ + □ + □ +
Item 5   Item 23   Item 41   Item 59   Item 77

□ = □ ÷ 6 = □
Item 94   TOTAL   SCORE

Faith □ + □ + □ + □ + □ +
Item 12   Item 30   Item 48   Item 66   Item 84

□ = □ ÷ 6 = □
Item 97   TOTAL   SCORE

Evangelism □ + □ + □ + □ + □ +
Item 6   Item 24   Item 42   Item 60   Item 78

□ = □ ÷ 6 = □
Item 95   TOTAL   SCORE

Apostleship □ + □ + □ + □ + □ =
Item 13   Item 31   Item 49   Item 67   Item 85

□ ÷ 5 = □
TOTAL   SCORE

Miracles □ + □ + □ + □ + □ =
Item 14   Item 32   Item 50   Item 68   Item 86

□ ÷ 5 = □
TOTAL   **SCORE**

Helps □ + □ + □ + □ + □ =
Item 15   Item 33   Item 51   Item 69   Item 87

□ ÷ 5 = □
TOTAL   SCORE

Mercy □ + □ + □ + □ + □ =
Item 7   Item 25   Item 43   Item 61   Item 79

□ ÷ 5 = □
TOTAL   **SCORE**

Giving ☐ + ☐ + ☐ + ☐ + ☐ =
Item 8   Item 26   Item 44   Item 62   Item 80

☐ ÷ 5 = ☐
TOTAL   SCORE

Healing ☐ + ☐ + ☐ + ☐ + ☐ +
Item 16   Item 34   Item 52   Item 70   Item 88

☐ + ☐ + ☐ + ☐ + ☐ =
Item 98   Item 101   Item 100   Item 102   Item 103

☐ ÷ 10 = ☐
TOTAL   SCORE

Tongues ☐ + ☐ + ☐ + ☐ + ☐ +
Item 17   Item 35   Item 53   Item 71   Item 89

☐ = ☐ ÷ 6 = ☐
Item 99   TOTAL   SCORE

Interpretation ☐ + ☐ + ☐ + ☐ =
Item 18   Item 36   Item 54   Item 72

☐ ÷ 4 = ☐
TOTAL   SCORE

Grace Gifted

Throughout this section you will find definitions/explanations drawn from a variety of resources. They offer insight into the meaning and use of grace gifts or spiritual gifts. After reading the definitions or explanations provided, read the passages of Scripture to see how the gifts were used in the early church. As an exercise, you might want to write your own explanation of the various gifts.

Definitions/Explanations of Spiritual Gifts

Leadership/Administration/Government
To set or place over. To be over, to superintend, preside over. To be a protector or guardian, to give aid.
Thayer's Greek-English Lexicon of the New Testament (p. 539)

To guide, as in piloting a ship.
Vines Expository Dictionary of New Testament Words (p. 508)

The ability to direct and guide a church with wise counsel in conducting the ministry God has given.
Spiritual Gifts Inventory (BSSB, unpublished)

See Acts 6:1-8; Titus 1:5; Acts 15:1-31.

Teaching
The special ability to study God's word and to communicate spiritual truths in such a way that they are relevant to the health

and ministry of the church and in a way that others will learn.
Spiritual Gifts Inventory

See Acts 11:22-26.

Knowledge

The ability to discover, understand, clarify, and communicate information that relates to the life, growth, and well-being of the church. *Spiritual Gifts Inventory*

The deeper, more perfect and enlarged knowledge of this religion, such as belongs to the more advanced.
Thayer (p.119)

To come to know, recognize, understand, or to understand completely.
Vines (p. 637)

See Acts 18:24-28.

Wisdom

Broad and full intelligence, used of the knowledge of very diverse matters. The ability to discourse eloquently of this wisdom.
Thayer (p. 582)

The ability to gain insight into the practical application of God's truth to specific situations.
Spiritual Gifts Inventory

The practical application of insight into divine wisdom to our own and to others' lives. *The Interpretation of 1 and 2 Corinthians*, Lenski (p. 500)

See Acts 15:1-31.

Prophecy/Prophet

One who speaks forth the word of God. The proclaimer of a divine message. The purpose of this ministry is to edify, to comfort, to encourage the believers (1 Cor. 14:3). Prophecy's effect upon unbelievers was to show that the secrets of a person's heart are known to God, to convict of sin, and to constrain to worship (1 Cor. 14:24-25).
Vines (p. 903)

The special ability to receive from God a message and then to communicate that message to others through a divinely anointed utterance.
Spiritual Gifts Inventory

See Acts 11:27-30.

Spiritual Discernment

The ability to discriminate between that which is of the Holy Spirit and that which is not, especially as it pertains to oral testimony.
Vines (p. 317)

The ability to know which actions and teachings that are claimed to be of God are actually of God (and not human or satanic).
Spiritual Gifts Inventory
See 1 John 5:1.

Encouragement

The special ability to comfort and encourage others as well as to motivate others to right actions.
Spiritual Gifts Inventory

To stand alongside another giving support and comfort—to console, to give aid to another. *Vines*

To address, speak to, which may be done in the way of exhortation, entreaty, comfort, instruction—hence encouragement embraces a variety of senses.

See Acts 4:31-37; 9:26-27.

Shepherding/Pastor

Tending herds or flocks—giving tender care and vigilant supervision.
Vines (p. 849)

The overseers of Christian assemblies. *Thayer* (p. 527)

Exercising care and control over others. The ability to build up, equip, and guide Christians toward spiritual maturity.
Spiritual Gifts Inventory

See 1 Peter 5:1-4; Ephesians 4:11-16.

Faith

The special ability to discern and affirm God's will and purposes in the world and to be a part of His intervention through prayer and the Spirit's power.
Spiritual Gifts Inventory

The supernatural ability to perceive the will of God and to commit one's self to doing it.

See Acts 8:26-40.

Evangelism/Evangelist

A messenger of good. A preacher of the gospel. *Vines* (p. 384)
The ability to comprehend the lost condition of people in the world and to present Christ effectively so that persons will accept salvation in Jesus.
Spiritual Gifts Inventory

See Acts 8:4ff.

Apostleship/Apostle

A sending, a mission. One sent on a mission.
Thayer (p. 65)

The ability to share the gospel in special ways. These are persons who are sent by God with His message of reconciliation.
Spiritual Gifts Inventory

See Acts 9:1-22.

Miracles

Power, inherent ability, used of works of a supernatural origin and character, such as could not be produced by natural agents and means.
Vines (p.757)

The special ability to serve as human intermediaries through which God works to bring about events that cannot be explained by natural law. *Spiritual Gifts Inventory*

See Acts 19:11-12.

Helps/Service

Abilities for rendering helpful services to the destitute, the sick, the persecuted, the troubled. Services for the sake of services.
The Interpretation of 1 and 2 Corinthians, Lenski (p. 540)

The ability to render service to benefit and help others, this being the only motive—all compulsion being absent. Helpful, voluntary service motivated by obedience to God as a servant.

The ability and desire to recognize day-to-day needs of others and to meet those needs personally.
Spiritual Gifts Inventory

Assistance rendered, especially to the weak and needy.
Vines (p. 317)

The ministrations of the deacons who have care of the poor and the sick.
Thayer (p. 50)

See Acts 6:1-8; Philippians 2:25-30.

Mercy

The outward manifestation of pity. Mercy is the act of God on behalf of needy persons.
Vines (p. 742)

The merciful person is to greet every opportunity for a merciful deed as a great find that makes him jubilant. Grudging mercy is not to be his manner of doing. We are to show mercy with great joy (literally, *hilarity*).
Romans, Lenski (p. 765)

Kindness or good will toward the miserable and afflicted, joined with a desire to relieve them.
Thayer (p. 203)

The ability to feel sympathy and compassion for and to meet actively the needs of persons who suffer distress and crises from the physical, mental, or emotional problems.
Spiritual Gifts Inventory

See Acts 9:36.

Giving

To give a share of, to impart (*meta*, with), as distinct from giving. The sense means to do more than to give one's physical or material goods. It encompasses that, but moves beyond it to indicate a sharing with others so as to spend or pour out one's life for others. Paul used this term in Romans 1:11 when he wrote that he wanted to see the Roman Christians so he could impart (give) some spiritual gift to them. He did not mean that he would give them a gift, but rather, that he would *share* or *impart* his gift or gifts for their benefit.
Vines (p. 489)

To share a thing with anyone.
Thayer (p. 404)

The ability and desire to contribute material resources to others and the Lord's work with liberality and cheerfulness.
Spiritual Gifts Inventory

See Acts 4:36-37; Romans 1:11.

Healing

Divinely imparted gifts of physical and spiritual healing. Carries with it the concept of wholeness, being made whole.
Vines (p.543-544)

The God-given ability to help others regain physical, mental, or spiritual health through the direct action of God.
Spiritual Gifts Inventory

See Acts 16:16-18.

Tongues

The special ability to speak to God through Spirit-inspired utterances and/or to receive and communicate an immediate message of God to His people through Spirit-inspired utterances.
Spiritual Gifts Inventory

The supernatural gift of speaking in another language without having learned it.
Vines (p. 1165)

Language spoken by persons who in rapt ecstasy are no longer quite masters of their own reason and consciousness. They pour forth their glowing spiritual emotions in strange utterances, rugged, dark, disconnected, quite unfitted to instruct or to influence the minds of others.
Thayer (p. 188)

See Acts 10:44-48 and Acts 19:1-7.

Interpretation

To unfold the meaning of what is said, explain, expound.
Thayer (p. 147)

The conversion of what is unintelligible into what is intelligible.
Theological Dictionary of the New Testament (p. 665)

The ability to convey a rational account of what was spoken in a tongue.
The Interpreter's Dictionary of the Bible (p. 672)

[Although the gift of interpretation is mentioned, no specific instance of the gift is given in the text of the New Testament. Some think that the explanation offered by Peter (Acts 2:13ff.) on the Day of Pentecost was interpretation.]

A Bible Reading Guide for Those Who Are Called to Stand

Your word is a lamp to my feet and a light to my path.
Psalm 119:105

Thy word is truth.
Jesus (John 17:17)

If you are going to stand in this hour, you cannot live on second-hand faith. You must learn to feed yourself on the word of God. Howard Hendricks put it this way:

> God wants to communicate with you in the 21st century. He wrote His message in a book. He asks you to come and study that book for three compelling reasons: It's essential for growth. It's essential for maturity. It's essential for equipping you, training you, so that you might be an available, clean, sharp instrument in His hands to accomplish His purposes.

To know the way of God, study the word of God.
To know God, His will, His way—know His word.

This brief guide is not a full course on how to interpret Scripture. It is simply a pathway to help you start reading, listening, and obeying so that you can stand.

1. Read with Intentionality

The Bible is written communication. God was intentional in giving it; we must be intentional in reading it.

The apostles believed that Scripture was:

- **God-breathed** and useful
- Able to make us **wise for salvation**
- A lamp in a dark place

From infancy you have known the Holy Scriptures, which are able to make you wise for salvation through faith in Christ Jesus. All Scripture is God-breathed and is useful for instruction, for conviction, for correction, and for training in righteousness, so that the man of God may be complete, fully equipped for every good work.
— 2 Timothy 3:15–17

We also have the word of the prophets as confirmed beyond doubt. And you will do well to pay attention to it, as to a lamp shining in a dark place...
— 2 Peter 1:19

God intends to be understood. He gave us a written record so that ordinary believers could read it, ponder it, and pass it on. You do not have to be a scholar to hear from God. But you do need to be intentional.

A few simple commitments:
- **Set a time.** Don't leave it to chance.
- **Choose a place.** Quiet enough to read and reflect.
- **Come with a prayer.** "Lord, speak. I am listening and ready to obey."

2. Simple Ways to Read
There are many ways to study the Bible. For the purposes of this

appendix, let's keep it simple.

You can read:

- **Devotionally** Select a passage or a book and simply read it, slowly and consistently. Let the words sink in. Ask: "What does this reveal about God? What does this call me to?"
- **Thematically** Pick a subject—faith, suffering, hope, the Holy Spirit, the Kingdom of God—and trace it through Scripture using a concordance or the cross-references in your Bible.
- **Chronologically / Historically** Read books in the order the events occurred. This approach helps you see the story of redemption unfolding. (Chronological Bibles and reading plans can help here.)

Whatever approach you choose, remember one basic principle:
> Any text taken out of its context is a pretext for a proof text.

Read passages in their surrounding paragraphs, in the flow of the book, and in the larger story of Scripture. Let Scripture interpret Scripture. Let the Bible shape your opinions, not the other way around.

3. A Starting Pathway for Those Who Want to Stand

All Scripture is important, but some books are especially helpful when you are trying to find your footing in a collapsing culture.

Here is a suggested pathway.

Step 1: See Jesus Clearly (The Gospels)
Start here:

- **Mark** – shortest Gospel, fast-moving, shows Jesus in action.

- **John** – deep, reflective, highlights the identity of Jesus as the Son of God.
- Then **Matthew** and **Luke** – to fill out the picture of His teaching, parables, and the story of His birth, death, and resurrection.

Read with these questions in mind:
- What does this show me about who Jesus is?
- What does this show me about the Kingdom of God?
- What is Jesus calling His disciples to do and be?

Step 2: Learn to Live as the Church (The Letters to the Churches)

Then move into the letters written to believers in the first-century world—a world every bit as confused and hostile as ours.

Suggested order:
- **Romans** – the most comprehensive explanation of the gospel and what it means to live by faith.
- **Galatians** – freedom in Christ vs. religious slavery.
- **Ephesians** – our identity in Christ and the armor of God.
- **Philippians** – joy and courage in the middle of hardship.
- **1 Peter** – how to stand faithful in suffering and cultural pressure.
- **1 John** – assurance, love, and discernment in a world of lies.

These letters will show you how ordinary believers are called to stand: in doctrine, in holiness, in love, and in endurance.

Step 3: Keep Your Heart Steady (Psalms and Proverbs)
Along the way, weave in:
- **Psalms** – prayers for every season: fear, anger, grief, worship, repentance, hope.
- **Proverbs** – short sayings about wisdom, speech, work, relationships, and integrity.

Many believers benefit from a simple pattern:
- One Gospel/letter chapter per day
- plus one Psalm or a few verses of Proverbs

As you get these essentials down, you can begin exploring other dimensions of the Bible. For instance, you could get the whole scope of the Bible from a chronological reading of the text. I taught *Introduction to the New Testament* in college. Many of my students had no knowledge of the Bible before they came to class (except maybe the exposure to sermon texts or Sunday School lessons). To help them, we spent the first few sessions looking at the eight periods of Old Testament history. Then, we scanned the inter-biblical period—before we ever opened the pages of the New Testament. That gave everyone an orientation to the story that unfolded in the ministry of Jesus and the letters to the churches. A similar experience might be helpful to you.

Step 4. A Story and a Promise
Dawn was Catholic. She came to a crisis of faith and decided she needed to move forward in her walk with Christ. When someone asked what finally helped her, she said:

> "I just took my Bible and began reading. Then I found a ladies' Bible study and met with them every week. That was the key to me moving forward in my faith."

Another woman said, "I determined to go straight to the source. I began reading the Gospels. I wanted to hear directly from Jesus how I should follow Him."

In both cases, the key was the same:
They opened the Bible and kept reading.
God has attached a promise to His word:
> *For just as rain and snow fall from heaven and do not return without watering the earth... so My word that proceeds from My mouth will not return to Me empty, but it will accomplish what I please, and it will prosper where I send it.*
> — Isaiah 55:10–11

If you will open the Scriptures, day after day, and yield to what God shows you, His word will do its work. It will shape your mind, strengthen your heart, correct your course, and equip you to stand.

Take up the Book.
You have been called to stand.
Let the word of God be the lamp at your feet and
the light for your path.

Group Study Guide Available

A free, downloadable Group Study Guide is available at **PGSPublishing.com**. The guide provides a structured, discussion-based formation process for use in churches, men's and women's groups, and civic study groups.

Get the companion volume—

The Battle for the Republic

Faith, Freedom, and the War for America's Foundations

THE REPUBLIC ISN'T FALLING BY ACCIDENT—IT'S BEING UNMADE ON PURPOSE.

If *Called to Stand* equips the warrior, *The Battle for the Republic* reveals the battlefield. It tears the mask off the coordinated assault reshaping America from the inside out. This is not drift or confusion—it is strategy: a generations-long march through schools, media, bureaucracy, and even the church, designed to hollow out the nation by erasing the truths that once sustained it.

Charles Garner names the forces, traces their lineage, and exposes how a free people can be quietly conditioned for control. If you feel your country slipping away, you're not imagining it. If you wonder who set the fracture in motion, this book will show you. And if you still believe the Republic is worth defending, this is your summons.

The walls are burning. The lines are forming.
If you would stand your post, begin here.

Available at Amazon, Barnes & Noble, and retailers across the nation.

Other books by Charles Garner

Beyond Expectations
The Kingdom No One Expected

What kind of Kingdom begins with a cross?

Jesus came preaching the Kingdom of God—but not the one anyone expected.

Beyond Expectations: The Kingdom No One Expected invites you into 55 vivid vignettes—each a devotional window into the life of Jesus and the surprising nature of His reign. From the wedding at Cana to the cry from the cross, these reflections trace the arc of a Kingdom not built on conquest, but on compassion; not rooted in might, but in mercy.

Blending pastoral warmth, poetic insight, and biblical depth, this is **devotional theology**—Scripture brought to life in ways both reverent and real.

Whether read alone or used a guide for Bible study groups, *Beyond Expectations* will draw you deeper into the story of the King who came to save...not the way we imagined—but just as God had planned.

**Step into the Kingdom.
Let it turn your expectations upside down.**

Available at Amazon, Barnes & Noble, and retailers across the nation.

Get the companion to *Beyond Expectations*...

Profiles from Paul
A Life Poured Out for the Kingdom

What Jesus began, Paul explained and extended—through a Spirit-empowered life of mission, message, and ministry. *Profiles from Paul* explores the story of the early church through the eyes of the man who gave structure to the gospel and insight to the Kingdom.

A devotional theology rooted in Acts and the Epistles.

In 75 short, reflective vignettes, the Apostle Paul's life is traced from conversion to calling, from mission to imprisonment. Each vignette includes biblical narrative, historical insight, original poetry, and questions for personal or group reflection.

Written for everyday Christians, this book brings Paul's letters and legacy into focus with warmth, clarity, and conviction. Ideal for personal devotion, small group study, or leadership training, this resource invites readers to walk the path of faith with Paul as their guide.

Available at Amazon, Barnes & Noble, and retailers across the nation.

It's NOT Adam's Fault!

A Decision in Carthage—

...over 1,600 years ago still shapes our world today... if you can believe it.

In *It's NOT Adam's Fault!*, the doctrine of inherited sin is questioned with clarity and conviction. What if sin isn't passed down, but is a personal choice? This book challenges "original sin" and offers a biblically grounded perspective on sin's true nature.

At the heart of this exploration is the Council of Carthage (418 AD), where the dogma of "original sin" was fused with infant baptism. What began as a theological decree became a power shift, used by the Roman Church to control monarchs, amass wealth, and dominate spiritual and temporal realms for centuries.

This wasn't just a doctrinal change—it was a historical turning point, one that reshaped Europe and beyond.

Through Scripture and church history, *It's NOT Adam's Fault!* reveals how a single, flawed translation altered Christian thought—and why Christ's freedom is far more radical and personal than we've been led to believe.

Are you ready to challenge what you've been taught about sin, salvation, and the gospel?

This perspective could change the way you see the world—and your place in it.

Available at Amazon, Barnes & Noble, and retailers across the nation.

Group Study Guide Available

A free, downloadable Group Study Guide is available at **PGSPublishing.com**. The guide provides a structured, discussion-based formation process for use in churches, men's and women's groups, and civic study groups.

www.ingramcontent.com/pod-product-compliance
Lightning Source LLC
Chambersburg PA
CBHW060455030426
42337CB00015B/1602